Praise for the Book

"Furnished with quotes, endnotes and a list of recommended reading, Sidra's unique contribution is a blueprint for Muslim women looking to traverse the trials and throes of marriage, relationships and living as a Muslim woman in a modern age. Sidra Ansari has written a lucid collection of advice that will serve Muslim women from all walks of life looking to make peace with themselves."

The Muslim Write

"In *Finding Peace Through Prayer and Love*, Sidra Ansari takes her readers on a beautiful journey of self-discovery and reform. Ansari's writing style, along with her obvious sincerity, give the feeling of sitting with an old friend and enjoying an intellectually charged and uplifting conversation about a variety of topics relevant to modern Muslim women living in the West."

Alaa Barghouti, *MuslimReviews*

"Ansari truly has a gift for providing solace to readers and encouraging them to be the best version of themselves."

Halimah Haque, *Words of a Water Lily*

"In the gentle and friendly tone of a trusted confidante, the author steers the reader through a wealth of advice for different areas of life with the aim of helping them find joy and peace within, even when their circumstances may not be wholly conducive to attaining it."

Nazira Vania, Writer

finding

peace

through

prayer

and

love

finding
peace
through
prayer
and
love

PRACTICAL TIPS FOR A SPIRITUALLY FULFILLING LIFE

Sidra Ansari

BEACON BOOKS

First published in the UK by Beacon Books and Media Ltd
Earl Business Centre, Dowry Street, Oldham, OL8 2PF, UK.

First edition published in 2021

www.beaconbooks.net

ISBN: 978-1-912356-52-2 Paperback
         978-1-912356-53-9 eBook

Cataloging-in-Publication record for this book is available from the British Library

TABLE OF CONTENTS

Introduction

Why Did I Write This Book?

I am one of you. I am a human. I have other labels too; I am a wife, a mother and a teacher. I am now a writer, alhamdulillah. I want you to know this because by writing this book, I do not wish to make any claims. I say the wrong things and do not always make the right choices. The idea behind writing this book was not to give you advice on how to live a perfect life, but rather, to remind you that despite imperfections, one can strive to carry on and attempt to live a joyful life. Life is full of tests, but these need not define you. I want you to know that in no way do I think I'm the oracle on the topics I discuss within these pages. I have simply picked up bits and pieces throughout my journey of life and would like to share them with you. And in no way is this a one-sided conversation. Please do check out how you can keep in touch at the end of the book. I would truly love to hear from you!

There are many reasons why I decided to write this book and I'll try to articulate them in the following passages. I suppose the thing I like doing a lot is meeting new people and learning about their lives. As a family, we have travelled more than most over the last decade and in doing so, I have heard lots of stories from people of all walks of life. I love hearing stories. Stories of loss, of hope, of despair, of love and crises; sometimes the ending is unknown and sometimes it is all too obvious where things are heading.

Through talking over many different scenarios, I've found that many of us get stuck on the same sorts of things. More often than not, it is the things that people feel they have no control over that they need the most help with. Sharing these stories with each other can help form a pathway to get through difficult periods of our lives. We somehow feel better knowing that someone has been through the same thing as ourselves. The fact that others have got through gives us hope that we can also do the same.

I truly believe that events that occur in your life don't have to define you. The meaning you attach to events create an emotion and this emotion actually changes your blood chemistry. Although you can't always change the events that occur in your life, you *can* change the meaning you attach to them. If you decide the meaning is positive and you see yourself, for example, as a Warrior rather than a Worrier, this translates into a positive emotion, which in turn allows your blood chemistry to work in your favour and helps you get through. It's an actual science! For this reason, my conviction is that one can manage a situation by changing one's perspective. The body-mind connection is so profound. One can actually change one's physical experiences if one changes their emotional response to the events that occur and this is the perspective from which I write. I have seen that situations will change, people will respond and things can move forward in a positive way if a past trauma is seen in this new light. Even yours.

If there is something you are dealing with currently, then there are two things you can do. Either:

- change the thing you can't accept by working through it, thinking up possible solutions and making a choice, or
- strive to accept the situation and try to make the best of it.

Intrigued? Chapter Four entitled Choices expands on this idea.

Where Did My Own Writing Journey Begin?

I began writing a blog in January 2018 and without consciously deciding it, many of my blog posts focused on advice on how to get through life more easily. This made me realise that I had a lot to say on the subject. Writing advice for the readers of my blog became cathartic and a way to make sense of what was happening in my own life. I began to write down three things I was grateful for at the end of each blog post and I was gratified to learn that some of the readers of my blog had begun to do the same. I had messages of support and encouragement and above all, I felt a huge sense of relief at writing things down. I felt that I had been carrying this information, these ideas, this positive perspective and mindful thinking for a while and finally, I'd found a safe place to put it all down. I felt lighter and everything else was simply a bonus. I would get personal feedback on how particular blog posts resonated with readers; sometimes to the point of the reader mentioning how they needed to hear what I wrote *at a particular moment in their lives* and how it changed their perspective and helped them get through. This was nothing less than a miracle. It felt like a sign that my advice needed to be out there at exactly the moment that Allah, the Most High, inspired me to write it!

One evening, at a social gathering, I received feedback on a post called 'I Used to Get Jealous' on the day that I wrote it in August 2018. I had actually considered deleting it that same day because rereading it made me feel uncomfortable and I wasn't sure that I wanted it in the public sphere for everyone to read. However, after hearing that I'd helped a particular lady work through some personal issues, I kept the post up. It made me feel that the posts were not there simply because I wanted to write them. They were actually changing lives. This was a profound moment in my writing journey.

Since writing over ninety blog posts on how to live life in the best way (you can read more and connect with me at *the7ofus. blog*) I felt, more than ever, that there was a way through this unpredictable, crazy, amazing gift called life and I hope that, after reading this book, you'll feel the same.

I have now come to the conclusion that the following statement will help one through life's tests and trials and will direct one towards a fulfilled life of gratitude inshaAllah. If you can't change something, decide to accept it. With a little faith, patience and acceptance you can get to a place of contentment, love and gratitude.

In other words:

> **ACCEPTANCE + FAITH + PATIENCE =**
> **CONTENTMENT + LOVE + GRATITUDE**

And when you have gratitude, my dear sisters, everything changes for the better. For Allah  has said in His Mighty Book:

*'If you are grateful, I will surely increase you
[in favour].'*
[Quran 14:7]

4

If you strive for gratefulness and contentment, in everyday life, that is where the treasure lies.

A note on contentment

I once overheard two people discussing how overrated contentment was. They felt that if one had contentment, they didn't have a true motive to achieving anything in life; they wouldn't strive to make things better because they were content. I think maybe these people were confusing contented people with those who are lazy! The opposite of contentment is not passion, and being content doesn't mean you are complacent. You can be both content in the moment you are in and show passion about achieving something in your life! You can believe you are enough in the state that you are, but also reach for the stars. The secret of contentment lies in the moment. If you feel blessed in the passing moment, as you are, knowing you are doing your best and taking the time to appreciate the small things in life—taking time to smell the roses—then inshaAllah you will find true contentment.

Now for a note on patience

Muhammad Faris comments in his book *Productive Muslim* that we need to be aware of being passively patient as opposed to being actively patient. There is a concept of patience that is required from ourselves, *whilst* we are taking the means to make a situation better. This is active patience and it is far from sitting back and doing nothing. Passive patience is sitting, doing nothing to change things (except maybe making *dua*) and wondering why things aren't changing for the better.

At absolutely no point in our religion is it expected for us to sit back and wait for change to take place. We are inundated

with choices in life and it is up to us to make the best out of what
we have got.

As Muslims, we believe the following two things:

*'How wondrous are the affairs of the believer! All his is-
sues are khair (good): when something good happens he
thanks Allah ﷻ, and his situation becomes even
better, and when something bad happens to him, he
stays patient, and his situation turns for the better!'*
[Sahih Muslim]

And

*'There is nothing that befalls a believer, not even a
thorn that pricks him, but Allah ﷻ will record one good
deed for him and will remove one bad deed from him.'*
[Bukhari]

InshaAllah, adopting this optimism will help us to get
through this life with astounding ease and peace. We also believe we were created to know and obey our Creator, to live in
harmony together and live the best life that we can in the time
and space we are given. No more. No less. Our religion is simple.
Sometimes we overcomplicate things. Let's strive to stay close
to the majestic Quran and make an intention to implement the
Sunnah as best we can (including complying to the shariah,
serving others and perfecting character) inshaAllah!

This book is divided into three parts. Part One begins with
my experience as a Muslim living in the West. I draw on my experiences living in different parts of the country after the life-
changing event of 9/11. I then share my experience as a mother
of five with a broken limb. Faced with one of the first physical

wake-up calls of my life, I turned to my faith, my lifelong favourite quotes and a positive attitude to help me get through. By sharing my experiences, I hope to not only guide people on how to deal with trials in life but also show how to adopt an attitude which will form the basis of a good life, full of gratitude. I then focus on how important it is to find something you're passionate about and how staying close to it throughout life, through making the best choices for yourself and living a life of appreciation and gratitude, will ultimately become mind-blowingly empowering. You will see an increase in all areas of your life. You will no longer be a passer-by witnessing a life full of chances and opportunities that pass you by without taking life by the horns and taking full advantage of them. After reading this part, you will set yourself free with the choices you make for yourself and your family. If you make a change in one area (to quote the personal development guru Rachel Hollis) like boats in a harbour when the tide comes in, every part of your life will also rise so that you can make the best of it, inshaAllah.

Part One: This Is Me, Who Are You?

Life as a Muslim Living in the West
A Wake Up Call
Find Your Passion
Make A Choice
Gratitude

Part Two focuses on striving to get the best from the relationships in our life. Even though sometimes, people and their actions are difficult to handle and may make us want to bury our heads in the sand and decide to live life as hermits, there are huge, life-changing benefits to having strong relationships in our lives.

Part Two: Dealing with Relationships

Ten Top Tips for a Happy and Successful Marriage
Maintaining Positive Relationships
Bringing Up Children in the West
Losing Loved Ones

Part Three emphasises the importance of looking after oneself. Choose to spend your time wisely and Allah ﷻ will inshaAllah put *barakah* in it and it will expand for you. Remember that ours is a religion of balance and allowing time for work, rest and play will help you to live your life in the most beautiful manner. Reducing time on the internet, healthy eating, exercise, stillness and meditation are also explored in the following chapters. The epilogue aims to consolidate everything I've discussed with one resounding message, to 'Trust in Allah ﷻ.'

Part Three: Looking After Yourself

The Importance of Self-Care
Tips for Time Management
On Dancing and Other Ways to Reduce Stress
Limiting Wi-Fi and Social Media
Healthy Eating and Exercise
On Sleep and Stillness
On Contentment
Epilogue: Trust in Allah ﷻ

At the end of each chapter, I am going to list three resounding 'take-home' points so that:

a. You are not overwhelmed by the content presented here to make practical changes, and

b. To stay in keeping with the overall idea that one can make simple changes in order to live a joyful and successful life.

I am hoping that after you've read this book, you will have learnt something new, heartwarming and inspiring. Above all else, I hope you'll be able to use these tips and tricks on a practical level and are able to navigate through life a little more easily. Remember to also look out for reading recommendations in the section at the back of the book.

Anything good that comes through this is from the Mercy, Bounty and Largesse of Allah, the Most High, alone and any mistakes are obviously my own.

I ask you to pray for myself and my family, that we are the first ones to take heed of any advice I cite here and that we are protected from becoming hypocrites. May we be a family of transparency—always striving to be our best, no matter who is watching. For Allah ﷻ is always watching! Right, grab yourself a cup of tea (unless coffee is your thing!) and let's get started...

Peace and Love,
Sidra Ansari
April 2020

PART ONE

P art One begins with my experience as a Muslim living in the West. It answers questions such as: What was I doing when we heard about 9/11 and why did this catastrophic event have such a seismic effect on my life? How did this event make me delve deeper into my religion and face identity issues that I didn't even know I had? Where did the journey that had me questioning my own beliefs and religion take me?

I then share my experience as a mother of five with a broken limb. During my childhood, I was named the peace-maker; not naturally inclined to make a fuss when I was hurt, either physically or emotionally. Sensitive by nature, I was hurt easily and was protected from any potentially painful situations by my parents. They would physically barricade me if I needed protection from my siblings, sometimes holding them down for me so that I was able to retaliate! So, as a grown up, going through a really tough period of my life and facing immense physical and emotional pain as a real novice was a huge learning curve for me. How would my positive attitude get me through this time? Surprisingly, I managed to paint a smile on my face and looked at all the things I was grateful for. My life was never the same again!

By sharing my experiences through this time, I hope to not only guide people on how to deal with trials in life but also how to adopt an attitude which will form the basis of a good life, full of gratitude inshaAllah.

In the next chapter, I then emphasise how important it is to find something you're passionate about and how staying close to it throughout your life will ultimately become mind-blowingly empowering. Trust me, you will see an increase in so many areas of your life. You'll notice that the passion which is ignited when you work hard to do something you love will feed other areas of your life. If you decide to prioritise this now it means that you will succeed on an unprecedented level, breaking barriers and becoming that limitless person you've always wanted to be. It is important to be aware that the opposite will occur if this area of your life is stifled. It will result in a lack of personal motivation and growth and will inhibit your ability to complete other things on your to-do list. Do not even think about sacrificing this area in order to free up time to complete menial tasks—the cost will be greater than the benefit. And remember, it's not always about making lots of money! Looking after your own needs and following your instinct in keeping your heart happy will help you to become your best self, always.

The next two chapters in the first part of this book dive into my two favourite life principles of making a choice and then mindfully sticking to it in order to empower you, and the idea that gratitude is the right attitude. Right, let's get into this.

Chapter One
Life as a Muslim Living in the West

To be a practising Muslim in this day and age is a tricky thing. Global situations can occur in the name of Islam that shift the perception of people and literally affect our daily interactions. We must adhere to the advice of the famous Sufi and poet of the 13th century Maulana Rumi when he said, 'Love is the bridge, between you and everything', and use love to bind us together once again.

And now to the day that changed our lives. Almost everyone will remember exactly what they were doing the moment the first plane hit The Twin Towers in New York. I was working in a bookshop and myself and the two other shop assistants present watched in shock and disbelief as the second plane hit the second tower on live TV. We watched as the chaotic scenes unfolded before us, our eyes watering in utter dismay and then shock as we saw debris flying everywhere and then, worst of all, we spotted silhouettes of people jumping out of the burning building. It was surreal; the only thing that desensitised us was the fact that it looked like a movie scene: the firefighters, the people, the noise, the newsreaders. It couldn't be real life, could it?

The second shocker of the day was that the psychopaths who committed the atrocity were Muslims and were doing this in the name of Islam. Islam? My religion? But why? When we'd been taught what a kind, just person our beloved Prophet Muhammad ﷺ had always been. Islamic history shows that there had been no fighting whatsoever until thirteen years after he received the first revelation and was given the news that he was a prophet. Even though Muslims had been unfairly persecuted in Mecca since the onset of Islam, they were told not to retaliate. And then, even when they did, the rules in battle were to *not harm women, children or any living thing i.e. animals and plants.* And most importantly, the Quran explicitly states 'that whosoever takes an innocent life... it is as if he has killed all of humanity, and whoever saves a life it is as if he has saved all of humanity.' Then, why? How, when we weren't even fighting a 'war', did these people justify the killing of thousands of innocent people? It was not justified, not right, and now innocent people had been murdered and innocent Muslims around the world had to bear the brunt of this calamity.

After this event, I looked inwards and began to practise my religion with more fervour than ever before. It may seem strange, but it seemed to me like the best approach as people around me started blaming Muslims and asking questions. Their curiosity and open condemnation of my religion caused me to research it extensively, and in consequence, helped me to renew my belief. A massive influence for me, and a lot of other Muslims in my generation, was (and still is) a scholar called Shaykh Hamza Yusuf. Through his recorded teachings of the Quran and sayings of the Prophet Muhammad ﷺ, I learnt traditional Islam.

What I would call traditional Islam falls under the category of Sunni Islam with a slant towards Sufism (Islamic mysticism). I found that whenever I wanted an answer to a burning question about creation or my purpose in life I was able to obtain an answer from a scholar who was given an authority (or an *ijaaza*) from a scholar who was taught by a scholar, who was taught by a scholar, all the way up until the connection is made to either the Prophet Muhammad ﷺ himself, or a companion who lived in the same era. The authenticity of such 'answers' was such that it didn't leave any doubt in my mind. The awe-inspiring knowledge that these scholars had and passed down to students ever since the outset of Islam is tremendous. When one studies Islam to any degree they realise that what they know is merely a pinprick in the depth of a sea of knowledge.

After 9/11, I found that traditional songs about Islam became popular in the English language; people like Yusuf Islam (the former Cat Stevens), Zain Bhikha and Sami Yusuf were a huge factor in supporting me in my new identity. I was able to wear Islamic clothing in public and felt strong in my faith. It helped me stay rooted, where I otherwise would have wavered. Establishing a strong connection to these fantastic role models helped me find my 'tribe'. People who were like me, grounded in a faith but also living in the West. These 'Nasheed' or Song Artists are still doing an amazing job of inspiring young people to be true to the Prophet's initial message of spreading goodness and truth. May Allah ﷻ reward them all.

After this renewal of faith, through obtaining Islamic knowledge, I began to separate the events that occurred from my religion. Not in my name. These actions are not connected to us or our beliefs. I was able to support the argument that Islam is actually a *peaceful religion* and contrary to popular belief *it was not spread by the sword*. Historically, many people of different faiths lived in harmony together in states taken over by Islamic rulers. There is no compulsion in Islam. In fact, if you were to visit Egypt or Syria, you would find very prominent churches which are attended by worshippers. All this talk of how the Christians or other faith communities were persecuted in Muslim lands is not without exaggeration.

> *'The history of Islam is full of examples of open dialogue between the Muslims and Christians, Muslims and Jews and even Muslims and atheists. The Christians and Jews lived an honourable existence in the Muslims states.'*
> [Habib Ali, a respected Yemeni scholar]

As I'm sure you are aware, in its doctrine, Islam is closest to Judaism and Christianity, being one of the three main monotheistic religions. All of these religions have Abrahamic roots and believe in only one God; but of course, in Islam, Jesus (may Allah be pleased with him) is believed to be a prophet and not the son of God, and Adam was our forefather and first man on earth. The message of belief in One God transcends time. Messengers were sent with reminders. The spiritual message of these Messengers was always the same. Everyone stressed the importance of God's love, obedience to His will, and love of his neighbour. The essential teaching revolves around the basic principle that everyone should treat others as they would like to be treated themselves.

What is a Christian? A Jew who recognised Christ. What is a Muslim? Simply a Christian who recognised Muhammad. We have more similarities than differences in our beliefs. After 9/11, having now started to practise my religion with a new zeal, I had different experiences depending on whom I met. Whilst living in London, I used to use the underground tube every day to travel to university at the time. I'd recently begun to wear the headscarf and this highlighted my beliefs to people around me. I would get stared at and was given a wide berth whilst travelling. Sometimes, people actually seemed scared of me. All the while, this made me dig deeper into my faith. I wasn't going to put myself through such hardship if I didn't feel a closeness to God and a huge benefit in doing so. In the stories of *seerah* and the Quran I found solace in the fact that many people before us had been ridiculed and laughed at for following their monotheistic faith. Indeed, the Arabs who were around when the Quran was revealed used to laugh at the notion of an afterlife. They used to say 'Who will bring us back to life once we have passed away?' Allah ﷻ says:

> 'A sign for them is the earth that is dead. We revive it and We bring forth from it grain, so that they may eat thereof; and We have placed therein gardens of date-palm and grapes, and We have caused springs of water to gush forth therein, that they may eat of the fruit thereof, and their hands made it not. Will they not then give thanks?'
> [Quran 36: 33-35]

There were also some funny moments on public transport. One of my favourite memories was when I gave up a seat for an elderly gentleman and when he thanked me he asked me if I was a nun. So sweet. He must never have seen a Muslim woman clad in her garments before but he recognised me as a woman of faith. It's a reminder that if people take a second to think about why we dress like this, it doesn't take much to reach the conclusion that we must simply be people of a faith. Forced, oppressed or emotionally abused doesn't come into it. I can't begin to tell you how many amazing women I have come across in my life that have been empowered and liberated by wearing a hijab. We are not bound by fashion or social norms to be accepted. If anything, it is an encouragement for people not to judge us by our outward appearance. By this, I mean our conformity to fashion and outward beauty, but by our inner characteristics.

Unfortunately, it is still very rare to be judged solely on what is within. People are more likely to judge us negatively for being an outwardly practising Muslimah! People often judge Muslim women when they do not take the hijab off. They think that if we truly were free and liberated and had choice, we would take it off when they asked us to. In other words, we are more oppressed by those people in the West who judge us for wearing a cloth on our heads than those who supposedly oppress us! I hope you have had more positive reactions to outwardly practising Islam, whether you choose to wear the hijab outdoors or not. If you don't wear it, my only advice is to try not to be one of those people who bows to the will of creation rather than the Creator. May Allah ﷻ guide you to what is best and keep you strong.

The future is bright. I am a firm believer that change is around the corner. With more young girls than ever donning the hijab, it will be difficult to judge us all in the same way. A very exciting phenomenon that has come about over the last few years is famous brands now selling modest clothing and headscarves targeting Muslim women. Hopefully this will increase the tolerance for our choice of clothing in the future. Truly, the advantage of living in a free country is being able to wear what we want without being questioned.

Beauty and outward appearances are only skin deep. How about we start a Women's Movement based on the fact that we should be judged by what's inside and not how we dress? This Women's Movement would see us being accepted for who we are on the inside. A Women's Movement started by Muslim women in headscarves—who would have thought it, eh?

We stand out so much, don't we? But we're not the only ones. I've often thought that as Muslims in the West, we stand out due to the way we dress and our beliefs. Maybe others stand out and are judged due to the colour of their skin, their status in society, their body shape, their disabilities. One of my non-Muslim friends took out her lip ring because she felt she was being judged by those who didn't know her. She would actually be treated differently by everyone, from her neighbours to the corner shopkeeper. Unfortunately, we are a society that judges people on their outer appearance. For example, people can become disillusioned and even depressed based on what other people post on their social media pages. For the first time ever in history people are able to derive a sizeable income from their own homes. Those who are the most popular in the public eye become more successful. Other people's opinions have never mattered more. No longer are we on equal planes even if we are all in our own homes. We constantly judge each other by our social media presence; outer appearances have rarely meant so much.

In contrast, to belong to a faith where we are told we are all equal in the eyes of Allah ﷻ is so refreshing. We can sit in our homes and pray and nobody has the right to judge us except Allah. Every little deed is worthwhile and will help take us to a better place in the akhira, with Allah's Mercy.

> 'So whoever does an atom's weight of good will see it,
> and whoever does an atom's weight of evil will see it.'
> [Quran 99:7-8]

This is more apparent on a trip to the Sacred Lands of Mecca or Medina. Families of every colour and creed stand side by side in prayer; it's a beautiful reminder of our equality before Allah. No longer bothered by societal barriers, we strive to be good before Allah. When we are misunderstood or things go wrong we can take solace in the fact that Allah knows the truth. There is no frustration, no feeling of being unheard or misunderstood—only a deep conviction that we are being held in His Divine Care and Mercy and that we are in Safe Hands. His Opinion overrides that of others.

One of my beloved teachers once said that whenever you are hurt by other people's opinion of you, remember that Allah ﷻ knows you. He knows your intentions and your actions, every one of them. He went on to say that if you can't seek comfort in what God knows of you then you're truly in trouble! And this should affect you more than what people think of you. You'd be better off using your time to correct this rather than worry about the opinions of people. I think this is something to remember when we feel too bogged down by what others think of us. Be yourself. Wear a hijab with pride and gratitude, or don't, but don't allow others to cloud your judgement. Life is too short.

I got married a few years after my priorities changed and moved to a small town up North and, coming from a multi-cultural part of London, it was a massive culture shock for me. I wasn't driving and would walk everywhere. I got treated as though I couldn't speak English. I got stared at, shouted at and even ridiculed once or twice. It seemed as though nobody wanted to sit next to me whenever I took public transport anywhere. Within a few years it ceased to bother me. Although I would be on high alert when I stepped out of my door, alhamdulillah, nothing serious happened and I got used to this ignorance all around me.

Racial abuse is relative. It depends where you live, how confident you are going out and whether you can choose to be less conspicuous. I decided to use main roads whenever possible and I preferred trains to buses when I wasn't driving. Once I started driving, I noticed that I didn't get anywhere near as much discrimination. I wore brighter colours and loose Western clothes rather than the traditional Islamic attire. This all helped a great deal. Recently I went on a trip to London on the train and before my journey I decided to tweet an organisation called Tell MAMA, who are doing a fantastic job 'Measuring Anti-Muslim Attacks'. I told them I was apprehensive and whether I should take any precautions before travelling. They advised me to be confident, be myself and made me realise that hate crimes were actually very rare. The media reports on hate crimes are disproportionately high and cause unnecessary alarm. I was very grateful for their prompt response and advice. Of course they were right. The journey went well and I could see that England was full of multi-cultural people and the only place I felt odd was the familiar short train journey close to my hometown, which I was so used to! It's important to remember to live our lives as normal. Media reports tend to blow the situation out of proportion.

Despite facing hostility and negativity frequently in my life, I was grateful for my first set of neighbours in the West Midlands, alhamdulillah. An elderly couple lived next door and, although it took me a while to understand his Black Country accent, 'Reggie' and I got on famously well. He would always have a smile and a kind word to say to me as our paths crossed and would always mow our lawn whenever he did his own, bless him. One day, we had a conversation in which he told me he admired my style of dress. He said words to the effect that it was modest and smart, 'much like it used to be in my day' (maybe alluding to the days before the war and shortage of material). I think it suffices to say that only a hundred years ago women in Britain were seen as 'loose women' if they wore their dresses above their ankles! I think dressing in a modest fashion and being British can most definitely go hand-in-hand. I loved how he was able to see beyond the labels that society gives Muslim women. He has passed away now. Having made friends with members of our extended family, he actually took the shahadah with my father-in-law. May Allah ﷻ accept it from him, and as he said one of the last times we met, maybe now we'll see him on the other side!

So going back to being judged by our appearances, it's a shame that some people can't see beyond the way someone dresses in terms of integration. I, for example, was born and bred British and I grew up in a loving Islamic environment. Our childhoods were spent building dens, strawberry-picking and collecting ladybirds, to name a few pastimes. We grew up with TV programmes like *Grange Hill*, *Neighbours* and memorable adverts for milk ('It's what Ian Rush drinks!'), beans (Heinz builds Brits!) and Quality Street (Magic moments!). I went to a multicultural high school in North-West England and then moved to London in my teenage years. I am not only fully integrated, I am immersed; this is my home. I don't belong anywhere else. To think that people have told me, other Muslims and no doubt those of ethnic minorities in Britain, to 'go back home', have judged me, are judging me at this present moment and will continue to do so in a 'free' society, is shocking in this day and age.

Sure, being a Muslim in the West has its tests, but overall I've got to say that I feel very blessed being a British Pakistani Muslim. We are allowed to cover and pray at work. There are no rules, as of yet, to restrict our dress and we are allowed to apply for any job we wish.

When we don't get a job, for example, we need to think that it wasn't meant to be. It's easy to think we are being targeted simply because of our beliefs and the way we dress. I always go back to the fact that I wouldn't want to work for somebody who couldn't understand or simply didn't tolerate my faith. Many Muslims (wrongly) believe that if they were to dress or behave a certain way that they would be more successful in this world. In short, they compromise their identity, wrongly assuming that the people who decide to give them a job (or not), have their sustenance in their hands!

There is a saying that the Prophet Muhammad ﷺ used to say that helps to remind us who is really in control. He ﷺ said to a companion, Abdullah Ibn Abbas, who was only thirteen years old at the time:

> *'Young man, I will teach you some words. Be mindful of God, and He will take care of you. Be mindful of Him, and you shall find Him at your side. If you ask, ask of God. If you need help, seek it from God. Know that if the whole world were to gather together in order to help you, they would not be able to help you except if God had written so. And if the whole world were to gather together in order to harm you, they would not harm you except if God had written so. The pens have been lifted, and the pages are dry.'*

This hadith is a reminder to hold fast to that which identifies you as a Muslim; have trust in God and He will provide. Even if the whole world got together, they wouldn't be able to stop the will of God. Destiny has already been written—nothing will change due to the actions of people around you. The decisions have already been made at a higher level. The choices are our own but our final destination is known. Don't despair! Allah ﷻ is with you at every turn. These people think they have power but ultimately if something good was to come to you, they wouldn't be able to stop it, subhanAllah. In truth, they are powerless.

Similarly, it's easy to think a certain individual has a problem with you, and were it not for that person you would be living a better life. Remember that ultimately Allah ﷻ is in control of everything. Nobody can harm you without His consent and this life was never supposed to be Paradise. It is full of trials and tribulations, and we believe everything happens for the best and that there is wisdom behind everything. In fact, we believe the road to Paradise is surrounded by difficulties and the road to Hell is surrounded by your desires. Control your *nafs* (ego) and strive for Paradise, even if it seems difficult; if your intention is to gain closeness, Allah will help!

Even if we can't see it at the time, in hindsight, we are always able to derive meaning through adversity. In this world, where our nationality, our faith and our colour may be used against us we have to remember that people don't affect our destiny. Whatever will be, will be.

I think what binds us together in the end is that we are made up of the same 'stuff'; we are all humans, feel the same emotions and go through similar trials on this earth. The least we can do is be there for each other when the going gets tough. Live and let live. Be open-minded and leave your expectations at the door. Chances are you'll find common ground even with the least likely candidate.

We have to be careful of when people become labels and stereotypes in our minds. The media hypes up certain groups of people but we have to be aware that each person is an individual in his or her right and has no right to be judged or discriminated against.

I hope that through my reflections in this chapter, you will agree that in actual fact:

'Mankind is a single nation.'
[Quran 10:19]

Much of Rumi's work reiterates this fact; he has also said, 'I am not this hair, I am not this skin, I am the soul that lies within.' There is more that binds us, as a human nation, than sets us apart. We need to remember above all else that the Messenger of Allah ﷺ was sent as a Mercy for the whole of mankind. A non-believer has a right to our mercy, compassion and love. We are mere human beings and, as one of my most beloved teachers said, just like dust particles floating across a shaft of light, winking in and out of existence. We are not here for long and have enough to do without taking it upon ourselves to judge others. Indeed, the Prophet ﷺ also said, 'I wasn't commanded to look into people's hearts or to split open their breasts.' We leave the judgment to Allah ﷻ. We all have until our last breaths to change and it isn't our responsibility to decide where a person will end up in terms of closeness to Allah. That's why we accept everyone with mercy for who they are, whether they believe or not and whether they (outwardly) practise Islam to a certain standard or not. Everybody has high and low *imaan* days—who are we to judge?

Three Take-Home Points for Chapter One

1. Let's remember to 'Be mindful of God' and that way 'He will take care of you'.
2. Mankind is a single nation.
3. A non-believer has a right to our mercy, compassion and love.

OK, that's what I have to say about identity. The next chapter will focus on wake-up calls; how it is so important to remain patient through a trial, how to deal with these unexpected events and how you might actually find yourself full of gratitude and peace after a bit of reflection.

Chapter Two
A Wake Up Call

This event in my life was a huge trial to see if I could live by the principles I fervently believed in—striving for patience through adversity by trying to remain positive no matter what. A real life case study of the equation I shared with you earlier:

> **ACCEPTANCE + FAITH + PATIENCE =**
> **CONTENTMENT + LOVE + GRATITUDE**

I guess I would say that a profound Belief in Destiny helped me to accept the fact that I broke a bone in my wrist in January 2018. My husband had gone out sledging with my four older kids and I reluctantly stayed at home as apparently it was too 'dangerous' (my husband's word not mine) to venture outside with my five-month-old. That day I slipped and fell on my side when I popped outside to put the bin out. This unfortunate incident took place just two steps away from my doorstep. No, the irony hasn't escaped me...

I felt and heard a crack as I fell to the ground. Or was it my imagination? What have I done? What have I done? I kept repeating this to myself as my muddled brain tried to comprehend what had just happened. One second I was taking the bin bag out and the next my slipper-clad feet had slipped on my icy drive and I couldn't even comprehend the impact that this would have on my five children, ranging from eleven years old down to my seven-month-old baby. Oh my baby! What was I going to do? With the baby asleep and nobody at home, my thoughts turned to how to get back inside. I sat on the drive, too stunned to move. Then I heard a gaggle of teenagers passing and through sheer embarrassment of being found on the floor, I managed to propel myself upright and into the house.

Thankfully, the cold and snow had worked wonders on my wrist and I couldn't feel a thing. Though somehow I knew, something huge had just occurred. I managed to walk to the sink in the kitchen and opened the cupboard where the painkillers were kept. I popped two in my mouth and gulped down some water. I then made my way to the front door again and grabbed some more snow from the porch. I held a clump of it next to my wrist. At this point I think that with the shock of it, the adrenaline and endorphins were running through my body so I had still managed to move around. I made my way to the landline in the living room, as I had no idea where my mobile was, and sat down on the armchair next to it. I dialed my husband's mobile and asked him to come back. When I hung up I began to feel a bit woozy and my left wrist that I held in my right hand began to get heavier and heavier. By the time he came back, five minutes later, I was not surprised that he said it looked broken.

I could call it a coincidence that I'd read Roald Dahl's account of his father's fractured elbow just a day earlier, but since I don't believe in random coincidences, it must have been destiny. The story goes that a misdiagnosis occurred via an unfortunate incident concerning a drunk doctor and a home visit in the middle of the night. His father's whole arm was amputated and he had to live the rest of his life with only one working arm. He consequently learnt to do everything single-handed. Roald Dahl reported that the only thing his father couldn't do was slice the top off a boiled egg! Reflecting on this story the following day in hospital, after hearing that I'd have to have my arm in a cast for six weeks, I felt doubly grateful that it wasn't a diagnosis to have to live without the use of one arm for the rest of my life!

It's amazing what a bit of perspective can do! Having a positive mental attitude throughout really helped.

And now to my favourite life quotes:

> *'Live life as though everything is rigged in your favour.'*
> [Rumi]

> *'Life is a journey, enjoy it!'*
> [My dad]

Apparently, these quotes can get you through all sorts of trials in life. So keeping my favourite life quotes in mind, I'm going to try to go through everything, putting a positive spin on my thoughts before and after this event.

- I am aware that it could have been so much worse. I could have been carrying my baby or it could have been my right wrist. I'm so glad it was an injury that carried the recovery time of only 6–8 weeks and no more than that.
- When the heavy snow was forecasted, I didn't want to drive in this weather. I had slid through it and nearly lost control of my car two years ago and didn't want to go through that stress again. Hmmm, must be careful what I wish for!

- I got an earlier and longer visit to London, where my sister had come to visit from abroad. Yay!
- I got a break from changing nappies (woohoo!). This lasted about three days until my eleven-year-old daughter proclaimed 'No more nappies!' After that, I learnt to do my best with one working arm and got adult help whenever possible.
- I could enjoy being looked after again! Last time was a few short months ago when I had bubba no. 5.
- I could make the most of a break in exercise and change-of-lifestyle type eating that I had begun just a week earlier with no guilt whatsoever (love this one).
- Everybody was very kind and attentive.
- To top it off, there had been deliveries of food, chocolates and beautiful bunches of flowers throughout the week from people and places I wouldn't have even imagined. Honestly, people can be so kind. It was a 'Chicken Soup for the Soul' kinda response.

And as if all that wasn't enough there would be:

- No school run for duration of cast
- No packing lunch boxes
- And absolutely no washing up!

Anyone fancy a broken wrist yet?

If you've had a broken limb and need inspiration to get through: Good luck! You will have bad days; just concentrate on getting through each day, one at a time. To take a phrase from Dale Carnegie's book *How to Stop Worrying and Start Living*, try to live in 'day-tight compartments'. Each day that you've lived through, your family has lived through and nothing awful has occurred is a success. Each day brings you that much closer to recovery. Acceptance of other people's gifts is a great form of generosity—squash that pride of yours and accept, accept, accept!

An amazing side-effect of having a broken wrist meant that I now had time to re-evaluate my life. A spiritual wake-up call if you will. How was I using my time? Could I use it more effectively to do other things? Needless to say, I wasn't used to a lot of time to reflect so soon after having a baby and it actually had a great impact on me. I started doing what I loved (writing) and reading useful things, both of which I hadn't had the chance to do for a while. After I passed three weeks, I realised I could move around a bit more and I decided to begin exercising every day and also watching what I ate. This improved my mood and the quality of work I was producing. It was incredible.

Now I can say alhamdulillah for this horrible event as it helped shape my life and priorities in a way that was very beneficial for myself and my family. If any situation makes you rethink your life and priorities and brings you closer to your Maker, then it must be good!

If you turn to Allah ﷻ in earnestness to remove your hardship and make your trial easy, if it is a means to renew your relationship with Him, then this trial that you're undergoing with patience and acceptance can end up being a really good thing.

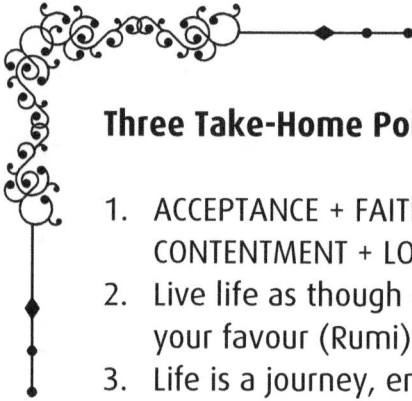

Three Take-Home Points for Chapter Two

1. ACCEPTANCE + FAITH + PATIENCE = CONTENTMENT + LOVE + GRATITUDE
2. Live life as though everything is rigged in your favour (Rumi)
3. Life is a journey, enjoy it! (My dad)

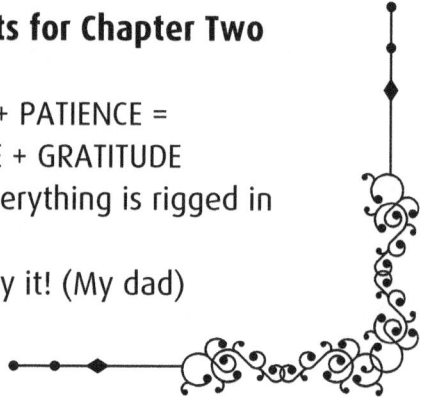

Amidst all this acceptance and positivity, life really becomes a joy when you find what you love. I am going to devote the next chapter to this. Read on to be inspired.

Chapter Three
Find Your Passion

A lot of people will identify with the fact that sometimes life becomes a series of habits or rituals. Sometimes, we find years have passed by in a state of half-existence. Thoughts barely go beyond getting to the weekend or the next holiday so that if you're lucky you can go and spend it with the people you love or visit a place you've only dreamed of. Do you look at other people in your life, and wonder where they get their energy and motivation to fulfil random tasks or to gratify such strange hobbies? Maybe their driving force is their passion.

The only way our existence on this earth is amplified is by changing our experiences; the places we visit, the people we meet and also the way we spend our time. Perspectives are changed in this way and our emotional response to events is also affected which, as I mentioned earlier, affects our blood chemistry.

Maybe you still haven't found that something that makes you tick; the action that makes you sit up a bit straighter; drives you a bit harder; the thing that makes you continue beyond exhaustion; the thing that you give time to beyond reason and with little motivation from external forces. The thing that when you're doing it, ignites the fuel to a passion you didn't even know existed. Well, guess what?

'What you seek is seeking you.'
[Rumi]

It takes a dollop of faith and lots of patience but you'll get there in the end. Because I truly believe that's the way it's been written. And then when you're ready, show some gratefulness to the One who put this beautiful gift in your lap, with a new and deep sincerity.

'Stay close to anything that makes you glad
you are alive.'
[Hafez, an inspirational Persian poet]

When you are glad to be alive, your gratitude will naturally increase, your sincerity will increase, your desire to worship more beautifully or give thanks via service to the universe will increase and this can only be a good thing!

We have to realise that success doesn't always occur in a linear fashion. The education system we have in place—nursery, primary school, secondary, college or sixth form and then university—maps out success much like a staircase, one step at a time to get to the top. Don't get me wrong—many people have found success this way and there's nothing wrong with that. But have you ever thought that there might be another way? The Steiner Education Philosophy uses the image of a tree as a metaphor to how children will grow and learn through education. I love this image and I feel it is a true reflection of the nature of any type of growth and change within a human being throughout their lives. Every child is unique and wonderful in their own way. They don't necessarily fit a blueprint but they will find success in their own way. They will reach for the sky, given the chance to thrive. I think it's really important to see the potential in people around us no matter what their backgrounds are and where their journey in life has taken them so far. People are gifted in different ways and it is our job to see and embrace that difference, rather than try to put people in pigeon-holes.

This is especially important when it comes to children. Maybe a child who is unable to sit still in class may end up becoming an internationally renowned dancer, like Gillian Lynne. (A quick note on dancing for women and the shariah. An all-female group or solo act is not prohibited if the music is not haram and the woman doesn't dance provocatively).

Her mother actually took her to a doctor because she was unable to sit still in class. In her own words, 'I even leapt on and off his desk. As they watched through the door he made the immortal remark to my mum: "There's absolutely nothing wrong with this child. You must take her to dancing class tomorrow. She's a born dancer." He was very clever. He gave me my life.'

There are children who can't sleep through the night who will be vigilant with their night prayers, children who don't seem to want to eat much who will be fantastic at fasting and children who can't seem to stop talking and sharing their views who will become world renowned scholars inshaAllah! An acceptance that we are all made to have different strengths and qualities means that we will be able to fulfil our potential in different ways. It's best not to compare yourself or your children with others or other people's children. Do what's best for you and them and don't be afraid to try a new path. Trust your gut. When you sit down to pray, use the time afterwards to sit on your prayer mat in silence and reflect. The answers are usually within you.

If you love doing something, the time you devote to learning it is not work—it's fun. And that's when the real 'learning' takes place. The hours you put in, the drive that you've shown in this particular field means that no matter what happens you won't give up. Many stories come to mind when thinking about this concept. We all know about JK Rowling being repeatedly rejected when she first wrote *Harry Potter*; likewise, Jojo Moyes, a contemporary author, had three of her first manuscripts rejected and then six publishers bid a war for the rights of her fourth! Once she was a published author, her eighth book *Me Before You* was a phenomenal success. Now she is an internationally acclaimed multi-millionaire author. The key is to continue; to just carry on because you are doing what you love. The rejection you face shouldn't stop you from doing what you love. In fact, most of the time when we are rejected it is simply because we are not ready. Don't take no as a sign of failure, but rather as a sign that there is a diversion ahead and to succeed, you must take another route. If a publisher picked up my first attempt of writing a children's book, I assure you, I would cringe as I read it today! In hindsight (and isn't hindsight a great thing in itself, subhanAllah!), I still needed to grow and mature as a writer, through practice (and rejection) before I got to the place I want to be. The message is that rejection and disappointment should help us to learn and grow and not give up!

It is true that what people see when it comes to success is simply the icing on the cake. The beautiful flourishing designs, the colourful fondant and bright candles. What they don't see is the hard work and effort that has been put into it to get there, the multiple attempts at getting something right (and the multiple failures to achieve this), the dedication, hard work, establishment of good habits, the disappointments, sacrifices and persistence it takes to reach one's goal. Countless authors have been reported as being overnight successes when this is simply not the case! Just recently I read about an author whose supposedly 'overnight' success took fifteen years of hard work and persistence.

This is why it is so important that once you find your gift, 'work hard' or rather 'play hard' until you are an absolute expert, and then use your gift to spread goodness and peace in this world. Use your gift in the best way you can and be grateful for it, and that, my dears, will be a fantastic use of your time.

Once you find your passion, life will have a greater purpose. Even better would be to use your gift to become closer to Allah ﷻ, to serve people around you and to find true contentment in life. Remember, to be content doesn't mean you haven't got any future goals. Your passion is well and truly alive and there is contentment in that. There will be no need to look for joy in artificial stimulants; you'll want to stay in the 'here and now' to fully appreciate and show gratitude for what you have.

Even though I've focused on monetary benefits here, I think it's important to note that even though working on something you're passionate about may lead to giving up your day job, this need not be the case. In fact, there are two scenarios here I'd like to share with you.

Once a lady came to me and said she fully agreed on my thoughts about 'Finding Your Passion' but, of late, she had become despondent; even though she'd been working on her creative hobby, she hadn't been able to derive a stream of income from it. So she stopped. I asked her why. She said because she hadn't been able to make it into a profitable business. I asked her whether money was what motivated her in the first place, and she said no. I then asked her why she would stop. The penny dropped. If your main motivation is not money but the simple pleasure you derive from a creative hobby, then you won't stop simply because you can't give up your day job. When you toil and persevere for hours and hours just for the sheer joy of creating, that is when the magic happens. Whether you make money from it or not, your life becomes that much more colourful. You are doing what you were sent here to do. You are fulfilling your God-given potential and there is a joy in that which cannot compare with anything else.

Own your happiness. There is a power in depending on yourself and your God-given abilities for happiness. When you derive happiness, satisfaction and contentment in doing what you love, it feeds into other areas of your life. You'll find that little things excite you, you'll be more open to living in the moment as it will help in reducing stress too. There really are no negative side-effects to this. Unless, of course, you choose something that is detrimental to your health to become passionate about or you become obsessed with your chosen passion and begin to neglect healthy relationships... at that point you may want to step back and rebalance things in your life. Balance is key, my friend. Of course, you might find that your passion lies in improving these relationships in the first place—to become a better mum, wife, daughter, etc. I am behind you! Do it. You'll feel better for it. Just remember to not get side-tracked by the Insta and Pinterest mums out there. They only record the good stuff. Trust me, they're not perfect either. That brings me to another point: *nobody has ever told you that you have to be perfect.* Seriously, where is it written that we have to be perfect? Just try your best and find peace in the fact that *you are enough.* You really are.

OK, the second scenario I wanted to speak about was something that was brought up during a conference I attended by Penguin. When speaking about how much an author makes, the resounding message was not to give up your day job. What?! I assumed that (post JK Rowling's success) the sign of a successful author was that you were able to sustain a healthy income level through your writing. I was astounded to learn that a lot of authors actually funded their passion for writing via a (sometimes completely unrelated) full-time job. Indeed, I recently saw a post on Twitter that asked writers whether they would give up writing if they won the lottery. The answer was an emphatic no. They would use their money to focus on writing instead. They would use it to live on so they could write all day. This is a message to find your passion and work on it for the sake of living your best life as your best self. Financial gains are secondary to this.

So, what are you waiting for? If you haven't already done so, find your passion and be grateful for the joy it brings you. Encourage others to do the same. Remember that your hobbies and interests are important and deserve time and recognition. Don't let anybody take that away from you.

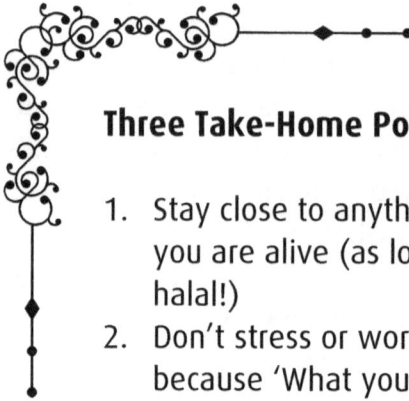

Three Take-Home Points for Chapter Three

1. Stay close to anything that makes you glad you are alive (as long as it's legal and halal!)

2. Don't stress or work yourself up about this because 'What you seek is seeking you' and it will find its way into your heart, because it was always meant to be that way.

3. Do not stop doing something you love because of lack of perfection. Just try your best and find peace in the fact that *you are enough.* You really are.

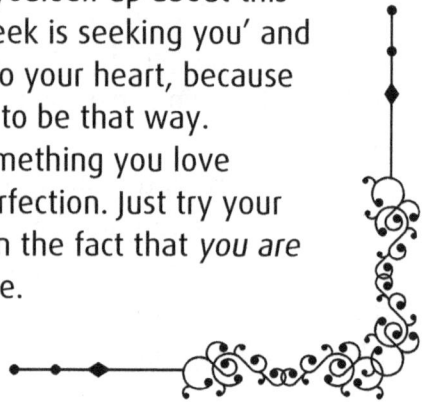

The next chapter focuses on the fact that we are given choices in life and not to become a 'victim' in the narrative of your life. Read on to focus on what you can change and become empowered by the choices in front of you.

Chapter Four
Make A Choice

Yes, we believe in destiny but does that mean we have to sit back, be patient, and accept everything life has to offer without question? Definitely not!

Beware of victimhood, dear sisters. It's when a woman feels sorry for herself when she is in a certain situation that she *can* change. Maybe she doesn't want to change it because she doesn't want to deal with the consequences of the change. It's important to *own* that. It's really interesting how your mindset changes when you realise that the situation that you are in is something you have chosen, rather than something you have no control over.

I'll give you an example. There is a woman (you may have met her in your life) who's absolutely fed up to the back teeth of working. She works hard at her day job and then she works doubly hard at home, catching up with the housework. Unfortunately, her hours sometimes clash with the time the children come home from school, so although she's happy that her husband takes over, she feels guilty that she is not at hand to feed the children and help with homework when they need her. I'm not saying that her husband doesn't help. He does the job well, but he doesn't maintain her standards—that's why she works doubly hard to catch up when she's home. She wants to leave work but she knows they could do with the extra cash. She feels stuck.

Do you agree that she has a choice? It is clear that she wants a certain standard in life and has made a choice to reflect that.

Now, there is another woman who has actually *made the choice* to be the breadwinner in her family. She enjoys the independence and freedom the extra cash gives her. She can now treat the kids when they're out and about and not have to count every penny when they want new clothes and toys. The choice is hers.

There are two things both these women can do: own their decisions and feel empowered that they can make a difference to their family's life in this way, or decide it's too much and try to come up with a solution with their spouses. If the woman's spouse is part of the problem, then she has to make the life-changing decision of whether she is willing to put up with this for her entire life. I'm not saying it's easy. I'm saying *own your choices.*

Tying the Camel

> 'The Prophet ﷺ was once asked "O Messenger of Allah, should I tie my camel and trust in Allah, or should I leave her untied and trust in Allah?" To which the Messenger of Allah ﷺ replied, "Tie her and trust in Allah."'
> [Tirmidhi]

We believe that although we can make firm decisions, certain things are still out of our control.

OK, so what does this mean? My take on this is that you must do *what is in your control*, and leave the rest to Allah ﷻ.

This acceptance comes from the fact that we know we can only make a decision on those things that are in our sphere of control. Huge contentment comes from this fact alone. You can only do your best, in any given situation. If nothing good comes of it, it wasn't meant to be and it wasn't through lack of trying on your part. When things don't turn out the way you have planned, you can take solace in the fact that you tried your best.

When You Need Help Making a Decision

We pray the *Istikhara* or the Prayer of Guidance, which helps us to make decisions. If the decision has already been made, then it is prayed to put blessings into the situation and make us content with the outcome, whatever it may be. Once the prayer has been done we generally look for 'signs' to help lead us to the correct decision. This could come in the form of a dream, through the lips of another person or in the way the situation develops (if there are no obvious signs initially). We are also told to make the prayer and put our total faith in Allah ﷻ to construe the outcome in the best possible manner. InshaAllah, it is the intention in the words of the prayer itself that lead to the greatest blessings and point to consigning one's matter to Allah ﷻ alone that leads to the greatest success.

Here is the English translation of the prayer:

> *'O Allah, verily I seek the better from You, by Your knowledge, and I seek ability from You, by Your power, and I ask You from Your immense bounty. For indeed You have power, and I am powerless; You have knowledge and I know not; You are the Knower of the unseen realms. O Allah, if You know that this matter is good for me with regard to my religion, my livelihood and the end of my affair then decree it for me, facilitate it*

for me, and grant me blessings in it. And if You know
that this matter is not good for me with regard to my
religion, my livelihood and the end of my affair then
turn it away from me and me from it; and decree for me
better than it, wherever it may be, and make me content
with it.'

As you can derive from the wording, the greatest secret lies in the contentment with the will of Allah ﷻ, no matter the outcome, knowing that 'everything is good' for the believer.

Ultimately our acceptance is multiplied when we consciously make an informed decision regarding our lives. Once we have this deeply ingrained in us, we will be one step closer to achieving our goals, especially those of contentment, love and gratitude, as the istikhara will help so much with the acceptance part of this fab equation to a good life:

> **ACCEPTANCE + FAITH + PATIENCE =**
> **CONTENTMENT + LOVE + GRATITUDE**

When we own the fact that our life is steered by the choices *we* make (that which we can control) as well as destiny (the parts which we have no control over) it will help us to form the left hand side of this equation. Acceptance is easier when we realise that we have done everything in our power to make the decision. Consigning our matter to Allah ﷻ is what will help with faith and patience. When the solution is known and the decision has been made, knowing that it's the best decision for us at this time for our deen, duniya and akhira is what will breed profound feelings of contentment, love and gratitude inshaAllah.

Remember that there are three ways a dua is answered:

1. Straight away
2. By warding off harm or an affliction
3. By something better given to you in the hereafter (which is said to be the best of the three) [Musnad Ahmad]

Also, in order for the equation to work regarding 'faith', it's important to look at one's relationship with Allah ﷻ. A good indication of your relationship is your prayer or salaah. Is it performed on time? Are you able to concentrate and connect? Is your income halal? Everything has a great impact on your connection with the Creator. Just as every atom's worth of good is considered in your account in the hereafter, if something is not right in your worldly affairs, it will also make a difference. My humble opinion is that we need to try to put it right. Whether it's not declaring all your income to the tax office or bearing a grudge for more than three days with a family member, it all affects your ibaadah or worship. Try to put these things right, repent privately and you'll see a greater barakah in your worldly affairs inshaAllah.

In dealing with halal and haram we often forget about our dealings with people. We get caught up in looking at how a sister dresses or at the length of a brother's beard. How about the way we deal with people? The Prophet ﷺ was known to have had the best character,

'Truly, you are of tremendous character.'
[Quran 68:4]

and we are taught to endeavour towards the same.

47

'The believers most perfect in faith are those best in
character.'
[Tirmidhi]

Prophetic teachings give us five ways to good character:

1. Fulfilling others' rights
2. Avoiding harming people
3. Being cheerful and positive
4. Recognising the good of others and responding with good in return
5. Also, and this is the true test, responding to the wrong of others with good.

Regarding point number five, I think it's important to reiterate the fact that to respond to somebody the way you'd like them to behave with you is better than 'tit for tat' behaviour. Giving someone a 'taste of their own medicine' can be very satisfying, but always try to remember that to take the higher moral ground would be to simply ignore the negative behaviour and treat people the way you'd like to be treated. This will inshaAllah have a knock-on effect of reminding the person of how one should behave. I think it's important to note here that this doesn't mean we should let people walk all over us but we should maintain a degree of self-respect and dignity in our dealings with people. Setting up healthy boundaries and limiting interaction with people who fill your life with negative energy and criticisms isn't simply permissible, it's actually necessary. Look after yourself and don't keep excessively close friendships and relationships with people who don't appreciate and 'celebrate' you. See Chapter Seven for more on toxic friendships.

This is all so relevant when it comes to making choices in life. After all, when asking Allah ﷻ for help in making the right decision, one would do well to scrutinise their interaction and therefore reliance on Him when matters in one's life are all going well. If we remember Allah through times of ease and thank Him, He will be there for us during difficult times inshaAllah.

> 'Recognise and acknowledge Allah in times of ease
> and prosperity, and He will remember you
> in times of adversity.'
> [40 Hadith Nawawi; Hadith 19]

I sincerely believe that the choices we make in life reflect our quality of life. Don't take these decisions lightly. Choose to prioritise Allah and you will not regret it.

Be a beacon for others in times of distress. Share the truth of Islam with people you meet by being a good person and always striving to be better. Allow the love that we share through being sisters in this path of Islam define the way you live your life. Do not allow anyone to stop you from being yourself, living a good life and having nothing but love for the people you meet. Strive to be yourself. Prioritise your need to be with Allah. Remain focused on Him and have a good opinion of Him in knowing that He will look after you, always.

I understand that some of you may be in terrible situations that you feel there is no way out of. If you do take things into your own hands, you may suffer great consequences. On the other hand, you may be dealing with a traumatic past that you can't make sense of. It may be difficult but realise that you have been put in that situation for a reason. InshaAllah, over time, you will see meaning in your suffering. It is part of you and your story; may you be emboldened by it and not weakened. May you become a Warrior and not a victim, or a Worrier. Only Allah knows why these things happen. Maybe part of the wisdom could be that you could help somebody in a similar fix later in life. Allah knows. We can only guess. Do what you can and leave the rest to Allah. InshaAllah, He is able to give you contentment no matter what your situation.

Indeed, we must also remember that part of maturing is going through difficult times in life. In order to grow we have to go through the hard stuff.

The Tree Parable

Once there was a tree, which somebody tried to grow in a greenhouse outside of its native land, but its branches didn't grow firm and strong like it would have in the wilderness. The environment that it would usually flourish in was replicated completely and they couldn't figure out what went wrong. Then suddenly, they had it. They realised that without the wind blowing hard on the tree through the cold seasons, the tree didn't build resistance or strength. In other words, without the hardship of having to withstand the wind, the branches remained weak and unremarkable!

From this we can glean that in order to grow strong as human beings, we have to build resistance; we have to work through the hard stuff. If we didn't we would remain soft and weak. Spiritually, if there is no resistance, one would stay weak and have no reason to progress and grow. What makes a person great is the fact that they've got through a difficult period in life. Allah ﷻ actually states in the Quran that we will be tested.

> 'And We will surely test you with something of fear and
> hunger and a loss of wealth and lives and fruits, but
> give good tidings to the patient.'
> [Quran 2:155]

Hard times are part and parcel of life. A spiritually strong sage would not only accept the hardships that come his or her way but would also be grateful for them. For the closeness to Allah ﷻ when one is suffering is second to none.

Thinking about some of the advice my parents gave us over the years, I know for a fact that for us to take it seriously and really learn, we had to go through it ourselves. It wasn't enough that someone told us second-hand. The real learning took place through our own personal experience. And now I'm learning this truth all over again whilst parenting my teenage daughter... some mistakes our children will have to make on their own. We need to pray really hard that they're not big mistakes. May Allah protect all our children.

Remember that nothing is futile in this world and justice will be done in the end. Every cloud has a silver lining. Allah ﷻ says in the Quran:

> 'With every hardship comes ease.
> With every hardship comes ease.'
> [Quran 94:5-6]

Scholars say the repetition here signifies that there are two eases with every hardship. Look for the blessings and you will find them. Shaykh Hamza Yusuf mentioned in a lecture I heard recently, that we seem to be oblivious to the many blessings that surround us because of the simple fact that we are human. That's the way we are created so don't feel bad about it. Just heed the reminder—we all need to hear it!

Concentrate on what you can control and remind yourself that this world is fleeting and will be over in the blink of an eye. The next life is eternal.

Whilst writing this, an Audible Show comes to mind, called *'What goes on here?'* by Sam Walker. It showcases many true stories of events that stem from adversity and reveals how the storyteller went on to have truly fascinating, life-changing results. The resonating message is that these people wouldn't want to change their negative beginnings because this narrative is part of their life story, and makes them who they are today. This is fascinating. It is a sign that there is wisdom behind everything we are going through and maybe we can help other people through our own experiences; all is not always as it seems. May Allah ﷻ help us to always make the best out of the situations He puts us in.

The overall message is that we can choose our state of mind. If we attach a positive emotional state to the events that have occurred, we can change the way our minds deal with this. Our blood chemistry (and yes, I do keep coming back to this) will change. If we choose to be Warriors rather than Worriers, chances are we can heal more quickly and help others at the same time inshaAllah. And don't forget, we must be 'actively patient' and work hard to change our situation physically, as well as waiting patiently for an opening and ease in the matter from Allah ﷻ.

As you have read above, there are many ways of getting out of a state of victimhood and taking decisions into our own hands. We have to remember Allah ﷻ is the Most Merciful and will do the best for us no matter what our situation.

> *'Never despair of God's justice. There is surely a lot that is wrong in the world, however, eventually, God will set things right; of that we can be sure. Quoting a 19th Century theologian, Theodore Parker, Dr. Martin Luther King, Jr. would frequently say, "The arc of the*

*moral universe is long, but it bends toward justice." The
suffering of so many innocents all over the world will
not continue forever. Wherever they are, one day, they
will be delivered from their oppressors. Live for that
day. Work for that day. Pray for that day, knowing that
the end of the circle is its origin and we were created to
live in peace. Do not allow anyone to lead you to believe
otherwise.'*
[Imam Zaid Shakir]

What a wonderful attitude. We would do well to remember this in times of hardship. To remain positive and believe that justice will be done in the end is a huge part of our faith, and this is ultimately what keeps us going. Belief in destiny and that God has a Plan will help us to remain calm and connected to the One in times of stress and great need. Trust in Him and you will not be disappointed. I will return to this concept in the final chapter.

Three Take-Home Points for Chapter Four

1. Beware of victimhood and remember to 'tie the camel'.

2. When making istikhara about something, examine your relationship with Allah, make it better and your outcome will be clearer and full of barakah inshaAllah.

3. Choose your state of mind. If we attach a positive emotional state to the events that have occurred, we can change the way our minds deal with this.

Next, we will look at gratitude and how appreciation of what we have can help steer us away from a life of materialism and the curse of remaining unfulfilled for life.

Chapter Five
Gratitude

Have you ever wondered why we, especially in the West, are so preoccupied with consuming goods? Keeping up with 'the Joneses' is so widespread at the moment that we even have an idiom for the phenomenon!

Where are the dishes and sofas that used to last people a lifetime? Many of us have parents who valued timeless pieces of furniture or decor and didn't see the need to replace them every few years. They lived with the philosophy of 'If it ain't broke, don't fix it' and the Post-World War II attitude of 'Make do and Mend'.

It seems that with the advent of widespread television and the innumerable plastic 'Made in China' goods (1930s and 50s respectively, if you're interested), goods became more and more replaceable and less likely to last beyond the two-year guarantee window.

How can we steer away from the trend that means we have cupboards full of toys, clothes, books, CDs, DVDs, electronic goods, you name it; houses full of new decor that is replaced every few years following the latest trends; phones that are constantly updated; brand new cars (some of which are paid for monthly and then replaced) and to top it all off, shopping centres that are still full of people buying more, more, more? It really is something to think about.

When my daughter was younger, I remember talking to her before a shopping trip about the perils of consumerism and marketing. I reminded her what we were shopping for and told her not to get sidetracked while we were out. At the time I thought it was a good way of making her think before she began asking me for everything that caught her eye on the trip. (This was a trip before pocket money and budgeting were introduced!).

'These people want us to think we haven't got enough. They want us to replace our things with new shiny things. They want us to buy, buy, buy while we are here. That's how they make lots of money,' I said.

About twenty minutes into the shopping trip, I spotted a beautiful dress in a shop window and backtracked to have a closer look, momentarily dazzled by the luminous sale signs on the window.

'But mummy, they're just making you think it's a bargain and that you need it! Remember, you've got plenty at home!'

Slap, bang, what a lesson taught to me by a (then) six-year-old! Don't get me wrong, I'm all for buying new dresses—it's a very important part of self-care and crucial to be happy in one's own skin—but accumulating dress after dress with no real purpose is something we should really try to avoid. And this reality is what hit me after that powerful reminder.

John Naish writes in his book *Enough*:

> 'We have created a culture that has one over-riding message—we do not yet have all we need to be satisfied. The answer, we are told, is to have, see, be, do even more. Always more.'

'What is the solution?' I hear you cry. Well, dear readers, 'We have to appreciate the unprecedented wonders now at our feet'.

So, with this in mind, I propose a plan to be mindful every day of what we *have* got. A plan to be grateful. Let's try to improve our mindset and 'develop a sense of enough'.

I'll start by listing three things I'm grateful for today. I'm grateful for:

1. My family—immediate, extended, big and small
2. A roof over our heads
3. Food in our stomachs every night

Maybe we could write a list of things we *need* and take it with us when shopping. Also, repeating this mantra to ourselves before a shopping trip might help: 'I have enough of everything I want!'

This attitude will help us a lot in this life, when everything seems to get bigger and better every year. From football shirts that cost an arm and a leg but become 'old' after just one season, to kitchen makeovers that cost thousands and then swiftly look dated. The way out of this is to go for 'classic' looks that don't date as easily. Go for quality products and classic decor that will last and withstand the test of time.

In an era of easy borrowing, try to resist. I'm aware of the strange looks I get when I make a purchase and decline a store card in exchange for a discount on the goods purchased. Who doesn't want a discount? Who doesn't want more time to pay for their purchases? You'll do well to remind yourself that the only reason the stores can afford to give you such big discounts in order for you to sign up is that fact that once you've got a store card, you're more likely to live beyond your means (and falsely promise yourself you'll get to it by the end of the month).

Live within your means. I know it's easier said than done. Think about cars, for instance. It's become fashionable to buy a car on credit and then by the time it's been paid off, it's time to replace it. I remember travelling on a bus a few years ago into town, and we were surrounded by brand new cars. An older lady remarked, 'It doesn't seem like we're going through a recession, does it?' This is very telling of our spending habits. Just because we have all the new gadgets doesn't necessarily mean we have a lot of money to spend.

Listing the things we already have in our life will help us to decide whether we need more material items in our lives. Also, writing down abstract things like the kind acts of other people, or the feeling that one has throughout the day due to different experiences will also be a very valuable way of living a life of gratitude.

Three examples of abstract things to be grateful for:

1. I'm grateful for the ability to understand what's important in my life at the moment and to not dwell on insignificant details.
2. I'm grateful for small talk with parents and teachers at school. I've read that small talk of this type can alleviate feelings of depression and loneliness.
3. I'm grateful for small kindnesses I received today. Lots of people smiled at me and gave me way whilst travelling on the road.

Being grateful for all the things you have breeds contentment and thankfulness and this is a very high status to aspire towards. We are taught that if we are thankful, Allah ﷻ will surely increase us. It's a win-win situation. We are also taught that if we look after our akhira, Allah will look after our present for us, so in fact, we don't have to get into this rat-race of human existence and can simply exist to please our Lord. He'll look after our affairs perfectly for us, inshaAllah.

I hope and pray that we remain grateful and try to practise 'enoughism' and mindful consumerism for the rest of our days.

This idea of enoughism or minimalism is a growing trend in the West now. Maybe the reason it's becoming more and more popular these days is that in this age of consumerism, some people are thinking more about the quality of items in their lives, rather than the quantity of them. All of our belongings take something from us, be it our time, focus, or our energy. With minimalism, we're practising mindfulness with what is taken from us and we are more aware of the belongings we own and how they affect us.

Minimalists love the phrase 'less is more'. Many people would like to de-clutter and hold on to the things that make them feel full and remove that which doesn't 'bring joy'. The idea is to focus your time and energy on what's important in life and this, in turn, will accentuate your most authentic self. Just like exercise increases the productivity of the body, minimalism increases productivity of the mind and soul.

Some may think this is a brand new concept, but we know that the Last Prophet ﷺ showed us a fine example of this attitude throughout his life. This is how he lived, even when (in the later years of his life) he was a wealthy ruler of a growing empire. Read the following extract which shows how he always strived to live a simple life:

'His house was but a hut with walls of unbaked clay and
a thatched roof of palm leaves covered by camel skin.
He had separate apartments for his wives, a small room
for each made of similar materials. His own apartment
contained a rope cot, a pillow stuffed with palm leaves,
the skin of some animal spread on the floor and a water
bag of leather and some weapons. These were all his

earthly belongings, besides a camel, a horse, and an ass
and some land which he had acquired in the later part
of his life.'
[Bukhari, Muslim, Abu Dawood]

Once a few of his disciples, noticing the imprint of his mattress on his body, wished to give him a softer bed but he politely declined the offer, saying:

'What have I to do with worldly things? My connection
with the world is like that of a traveller resting for a while
underneath the shade of a tree and then moving on.'

His wife Aisha (may Allah be pleased with her) said that there was hardly a day in his life when he had two square meals [Sahih Muslim]. What a great example of simplicity and 'enoughism'!

A moment of reflection will serve one well to decide to change one's perspective. If we're always comparing ourselves to people who have bigger and better, we'll always fall short. Regarding the duniya, the trick is to look to those who have less. Then we'll realise what we've got. (In contrast, regarding the deen, we always aspire to those who have more, in terms of closeness to Allah ﷻ.)

In fact, if we have food in our stomachs, a warm house to live in all year round and a wi-fi connection, we are amongst the richest ten percent of the population of the world!

Remember the equation:

> **ACCEPTANCE + FAITH + PATIENCE =**
> **CONTENTMENT + LOVE + GRATITUDE**

Gratitude is a consequence of showing faith, acceptance and patience in a situation. If it is present in every corner of your life, it is an indicator that you have these traits well and truly realised in your life and you are on your way to living a life full of peace, prayer and love. It also helps one stay away from despair and depression, so if this is you, well done!

Mental health is a huge topic right now as it's come to the forefront in many contemporary discussions. Lots of celebrities have admitted to having mental health problems and this has led to greater acceptance and less taboo surrounding this subject, which is fantastic. Many studies have been done to show that gratitude increases happiness and therefore reduces depression. A solution for someone who is feeling depressed is to list things one is grateful for every morning. Another useful take on this would be to make a collage which represents everything one is grateful for in life and reflect upon this when one is feeling low and it is said to help a great deal. I think it's important to mention here that there is a difference between the mental health issues that require professional help and a low level bout of depression. If you have symptoms of the former, the best thing to do would be to go your GP and he or she will decide the best course of action for you.

Why being grateful helps with a low period in your life:

- Research shows that gratitude reduces the stress hormone and significantly increases the feel-good hormone.
- Deciding to be grateful makes one happy. The choice made is a step in the right direction and signals fifty percent of success already. This is because gratitude means noticing small kindnesses and will safeguard against self-absorption; heightening our perception of the goodness in the world will help in our appreciation of it.

- Feeling grateful brings emotions such as awe, wonder, happiness and joy and these feelings push depression aside.
- Gratitude helps so much to give one positive emotions and strength which means one will increase their willpower to do other great things in life.
- Random acts of kindness: to proactively go out and seek acts of kindness for family, friends and strangers and help to make a difference in their lives reduces depressive thoughts in one's own life. Serving others has always been a foundational part of our deen and this is a beautiful way that this behaviour is rewarded.
- Gratitude increases our closeness to Allah ﷻ. It turns what we have into enough! It attracts more good things into our life. Recognise goodness breeds goodness and the opposite is true.

The topics I have spoken about so far in this book all have an effect on gratitude. One's identity, one's passion and the choices one makes all affect the ultimate gratitude one has in life, in one's Maker and the life one ends up with. Being grateful towards one's Creator is a huge part of being a Muslim and a high spiritual station to aspire towards.

During one particular nighttime prayer, the Prophet Muhammad ﷺ prayed and wept. When the Prophet Muhammad ﷺ was asked by Aisha, his wife, 'O Messenger of Allah, what causes you to weep, when Allah ﷻ has forgiven you your earlier and later sins?' He ﷺ replied: 'Should I not be a thankful servant?' This indicates how important it is to show gratefulness to Our Creator for everything He has ever done for us. We can show our gratefulness by increasing our sincerity during acts of worship like standing in prayer.

Thankfulness can take many different forms:

1. Gratitude of the tongue: To acknowledge one's blessings with a humble heart.
2. Gratitude of the body and the limbs: Loyalty and a life of servitude.
3. Gratitude of the heart: This requires a careful balance between the visible display of appreciation and the constant preservation of a sense of reverence.
4. Gratitude of the eyes: To overlook any fault you notice in your companion.
5. Gratitude of the ears: To ignore any fault you hear him accused of possessing.

In the simplest terms, thankfulness means that you do not disobey Allah (Exalted is He) by not using His gracious favours as they were meant to be used.

> 'My God, how can I thank You, when my thankfulness
> to You is itself a blessing from among Your gracious
> favours?' The Prophet David once said.
> Allah (Blessed and Exalted is He) conveyed to him by
> way of inspiration: 'Now you have thanked Me indeed!'

SubhanAllah. To be grateful is in itself a great blessing to be thankful for.

Three Take-Home Points for Chapter Five

1. Adopt an attitude that says 'I have enough!' by being grateful for the things you already have in your life, for a state of gratitude is a high station to attain.

2. The Prophet ﷺ was the best example in minimalism hundreds of years before it came into fashion; he wanted nothing to do with worldly things.

3. Feeling grateful brings emotions such as awe, wonder, happiness and joy and these feelings push depression aside.

I hope it's been useful getting to know the fundamental aspects of gratitude in this last chapter. InshaAllah it will help you to remain thankful, knowing that we always have a lot to be grateful for. If you're going through a bad patch in your life, listing all the things you are grateful for regularly, every morning as soon as you wake up, is a great way to change your perspective.

PART TWO

Part Two focuses on striving to get the best from the relationships in our life. It begins with the all-important marital relationship and then shifts to friendships, children and then that utterly devastating point when relationships, the great stories we never expected to end, do sadly face their final chapter through death.

The first chapter in this part of the book is the result of a lot of research and conferring with women whom I felt were very successful in this regard. I know that sometimes marital advice can feel overwhelming and difficult to successfully implement, so this chapter contains valuable titbits of information condensed down to Ten Top Tips. I hope you find it useful.

The chapter on friendship contains the message that even though people and their actions are difficult to handle sometimes, and we may feel like running and hiding, living the life of a recluse is not really a viable option (trust me, at post thirty-five years of age I've thought about this a lot!). Therefore, it is so important to learn how to maintain strong relationships in our lives. I discuss 'toxic friends'; how to recognise a toxic friendship and how to protect yourself from its negative effects. It took me many years to decide to avoid these kinds of people in my life. My parents had always taught me to give people the benefit of the doubt and 'make seventy excuses for the believer'; however, now I'm a huge advocate for reading the signs and not giving that person the time of day. Don't get me wrong, we should still give people the benefit of the doubt and therefore all our love, but when a person proves that they deserve other than your respect and kindness through showing toxic traits, it's important to notice this and take a step back. Despite this, we must be aware that many people may have noble intentions. Read about how you can distinguish the two and make the best choice for yourself.

In discussing our children, I am the first to admit that this is a bumpy road full of unprecedented ups and downs. It's very subjective; every parent I know goes through a truly unique experience, according to their own upbringing and expectations, and other external factors such as their environment, influence (and support) of extended family members, friends and differing discipline levels. I've outlined the advantages of home education according to our own experiences and the importance of reading up on parenting books to grow and progress as parents.

After this, I turn to the topic of losing close family members and friends and how to deal with the end of relationships in this world. To focus on the next life is paramount in acceptance and this is what I discuss here, amongst other reminders.

Let's begin with marriage.

Chapter Six
Ten Top Tips for a Happy and Successful Marriage

I love the idea of a hierarchy of those who deserve your love and respect. Allah, the Most High, is at the top, then our Beloved Messenger ﷺ next, then one's husband, children, parents, immediate family and teachers; then closest friends and extended family; then the greater community. When the order of priority is mixed up, the foundation is unstable; there isn't peace in the home and this may be a huge reason why children can become rebellious. The concentric circles of concern within which we live must be examined—an awareness of Allah ﷻ is essentially at the top of the pyramid and then that barakah will run through to all other relationships, like the blood coursing through our veins. This is vital for healthy relationships.

Therefore, throughout this book, we closely examine and try to emphasise improving our relationship with Allah ﷻ. Next, especially when striving to lead a good life, it is imperative to closely examine and maintain a loving relationship with the Messenger of Allah ﷺ. Through his perfect example we can learn how to conduct relationships and serve the Most Merciful with gratitude and love. Then, the one long-term relationship within humankind in this duniya is in a marriage with one's spouse. I'm sure you'll agree that it is, at once, the most life-changing, challenging and ultimately, the most rewarding partnership of all.

When things are not working in a marriage, it is natural to look to those of us who have more experience in these matters. Maybe you would look to your own parents, or an aunty or uncle who have remained married for a number of years? However, sometimes family members are too close to ask advice from—maybe you know too much or maybe not anywhere near enough in order to learn from them. For the writing of this chapter I asked many women, whom I highly respect and admire, for their advice and input on the subject and through all this discovery, I put together ten top tips. I hope you learn something new and enjoy applying it to your marriage! I certainly benefit from rereading these tips every now and again as I'll be the first to admit, I'm not a perfect wife, nor do I have a perfect marriage.

Why You?

A modern Muslim woman plays a myriad of roles, both within the household and outside. Although, with a wonderful role model like Sayyidina Khadija, who was a businesswoman at the time of her marriage with our beloved Prophet ﷺ, I don't see why this is seen as a modern rather than a traditional role. Anyhow, some women these days seem to want it all—a full family home and work outside the household too. Others don't seem to have a choice in the matter; not only are they expected to work outside the house to cover household expenses, they are also required to carry out menial chores in the house.

With so many roles and duties pulling us from multiple directions, is it a wonder that we're finding it difficult to fulfil our responsibilities as married women?

Before we begin the top ten, there is a very important concept that came through whilst researching great marriages. Many, many couples who have seen success in this area have done so because they are:

CONSTANTLY WORKING AT IT!

A very wise woman and beloved teacher once said, 'If you're not working on your marriage, it's not working!' This is a reminder to not sit back on our laurels and expect everything to fall into place. One must always be willing to respond differently if the situation calls for it. This statement also suggests that it is our duty to find out how to correct our behaviour, expectations and attitude if things aren't going well in our marriages. In it is a subtle reminder that we have to work at something in order to be successful! And may Allah, the Most High, give us all success on this front, ameen.

So, let's begin.

1. Meeting Emotional Needs

Emotional needs are not to be ignored. The primary emotional need of a woman is to be loved and of a man is to be respected.

> 'To make a woman feel loved give her the three AAAs:
> Attention, Affection, & Appreciation. To make a man
> feel loved give him the three RRRs: Respect,
> Reassurance, & Relief.'
> [Laura Doyle]

It is imperative that the husband and wife ensure each other's happiness on a general level—this will increase levels of intimacy too. When the physical and emotional needs of each spouse is met, intimacy thrives on all levels. When a man meets a woman's needs she will happily fulfil his sexual desires. When a woman meets a man's needs he will work harder to give her affection, love and appreciation. Taking care of each other's physical and emotional needs is highly beneficial to both of you.

Another book, *The Proper Care and Feeding of Husbands* by Laura Schlessinger states that men are very simple creatures and they actually crave *respect* more than physical intimacy. But how do we respect a being that doesn't give the baby her milk when she is left in his care for an hour or two, even though it was left made and cooling on the counter top? 'But she didn't need it, she was happy!' comes the reply.

Well my friends, we take a deep breath and try to be thankful that at least you can leave the baby safely, that she does seem happy enough, that he did volunteer himself to take care of the baby while you went out/had a shower/had a nap, etc. So I guess what I'm saying is, we need to practise 'enoughism' with our husbands. We have to be thankful for the qualities they do possess, rather than be wistful for the ones they don't! We mustn't compare with other husbands (especially not out loud!) and we most certainly should thank them (very loudly!) for everything they *do* do.

2. Expectations and Acceptance

We should take a look at how you've both been brought up because that really does make a difference to one's expectations in a marriage. When expectations are not met, that's when people are disappointed. If you're not married, think about going through basic expectations like where you'll live; who will be living under the same roof (very important question for many Pakistanis!); how the living costs will be divided; whether you want a family; when you will begin trying, etc. Discuss these things (and more) with someone you wish to spend the rest of your life with and when you go in knowingly, hopefully you will not be disappointed. Compromise and Sacrifice are two big words to think about here.

Remember the famous Christian Serenity prayer?

> '*God, grant me the serenity to accept*
> *the things I cannot change,*
> *Courage to change the things I can,*
> *And wisdom to know the difference.*'

We can apply it within our marriage. It is crucial to consider the choices you have made and whether you can live with them for life.

3. Self-Care

It is so important to look after yourself, so that you can always be your *best self* for your spouse. This means inside and out. It's very interesting that we tend to dress up to go *out*, not realising that the people we live with also deserve to see us looking (not to mention behaving) in the best possible way.

Cleanliness is half of our faith. Keeping up a basic neat appearance is essential to a good marriage.

> '*Keeping clean is half of faith.*'
> [Muslim]

Too many people follow the protocol of looking good whilst they're outside and lounging about in their PJs when they're at home. It's all very well having comfortable clothing but it's also important to choose lovely clothes for inside the home too. Ladies, this is our arena! Use the space to be feminine and feel good about yourself at the same time. Get your hair done, a mani, a pedi, or whatever it is that makes you feel like a lady. You deserve it! When you look after yourself and your surroundings too, you will feel infinitely better about the work you have to do, whether you work outside the home or in it.

'Allah loves those who turn to him, and loves those who keep themselves clean.'
[Quran 2:222]

Self-care is so important that I've dedicated a whole chapter to it (see Chapter 10). It is so much easier to be a good wife if you look after yourself first. Sometimes there's absolutely no time for it; be honest and let your husband know that you're exhausted and looking forward to some 'me time' as soon as the opportunity arises. That way he knows to take time out to watch the kids and hopefully give you time to do something for yourself. Don't forget it's in his own interest too. He wants a happy wife! See point six below.

4. Remind Men of Their Masculinity

Remember that we have to let men know that we think they're strong and capable and able to look after us. We have to let them know that we rely on them for protection and support and couldn't do without them. *We need to make sure they know they're needed.* It's all very well being independent and able to control our own lives and happiness but a man likes to feel that you can't get on without him. We all end up doing odd jobs around the house, for example, putting the bins out, mending drawers and fixing locks, but to ask hubby to do it (in a feminine way) makes him assume his role of man of the house and makes him feel more masculine and 'needed'. Also, it is imperative to refrain from dialogue that shuts him out, like 'I feel like a single parent!' or 'What do you do anyway? We're better off without you!'. These are examples of foul and poisonous things to say to your spouse. By having the responsibility of being the main earner of the family, the husband carries a huge responsibility on his shoulders. If he does this well, he should have already earned your respect—everything else he contributes towards the household is a bonus.

I'm aware that this may cause some controversy, especially from those women who don't feel the need to resort to 'traditional' roles in a marital situation. OK, that's fine. No problem. This opinion has been drawn from my own perspective of seeing a LOT of successfully married couples who *have* resorted to these roles. When a woman decides to be the main breadwinner for the household, she will still be able to turn on her feminine charm so that she doesn't end up doing everything to maintain the household too. It certainly isn't unislamic for a man to help around the home.

Aisha, the wife of the Prophet Muhammad ﷺ, was asked,

> *'What did the Prophet used to do in his house?' She*
> *replied, 'He used to keep himself busy serving his family*
> *and when it was the time for prayer he would go for it.'*
> [Bukhari]

A wonderful Islamic trait of a man is that he is active in helping to run the household in partnership with his wife. I think the key is to appreciate everything he does and to not criticise him, even if he isn't completing tasks to your standard. This way, he'll be happy to help and will even feel his worth increase. You will only push him away if you complain that he never does things right and you will find that you'll take all the enjoyment out of completing household tasks together. This is a time to use duct tape, ladies. Accept help and don't complain about what doesn't get done properly! InshaAllah you'll find you have a partner within the household, for life!

Neither is it unislamic for a lady to work outside the home. Indeed, our mother Sayyidina Khadija (may Allah be pleased with her) was a highly successful businesswoman and a great example for us all to follow but no matter how much we earn, we must concede to the fact that the man is the head of the household and, (wait for it) the woman is the neck. That is to say, she certainly has a big say in the household decisions that are made but she uses subtlety and diplomacy to get what she needs rather than force. This way the man still thinks he's in charge. And everyone's happy. (I hope my husband doesn't read this part. Haha.)

A little note here to say that, even within the analogy of being the neck of the household, we have to admit that our husband has *the final word* on all household decisions. There is great wisdom in this in that once we have had our say in a matter, it is up to him to make the final decision, we can sit back and relax and put our trust in Allah that we have done our best. It has to be this way, because otherwise the two chiefs would always be at loggerheads with each other! In my own experience, I can say that I have found a lot of barakah in listening to my husband when I don't agree with him, and I've found a lack of barakah when I don't! Enough to make me work on always trying to listen in the best way. I therefore need to stamp on my nafs, and remind you to do the same in these matters.

5. Communication

Communication is, of course, key to a good relationship (with anyone). Always try to talk about things that are bothering you in a calm and collected manner. There isn't any point discussing things:

a. When things are heated and one or both of you are angry
b. In front of the children
c. When one or both of you are tired
d. When one or both of you have just come back from work

Wait for a time when you're both relaxed, calm and not likely to be distracted and try to keep 'blame' out of the conversation. How you speak to your husband helps too. For example, '*I need you* to help me with the children...' rather than 'Take them away from me! Now!'

Also, try to turn conversations around to remain positive... 'We miss you' rather than 'Why are you always out?' really helps. Try to begin sentences with the pronouns 'I' and 'we' and you should be off to a good start.

Character, too, is crucial. Muslims believe that *even a smile is charity* and *charity begins at home.* Give your spouse, your children and the people you live with a smile every day (at least!). A beautiful characteristic of Prophet Muhammad ﷺ was that when someone used to talk to him, he would turn *fully* towards them and listen. I've tried to do this in my home. I've noticed it's difficult to do, especially when carrying out a task. When I remember to do this I can see the recipient lights up from inside—they really bask in the warmth of my attention and love.

It is so important for a man to try his utmost to listen to his wife, to simply listen, without feeling angry or becoming defensive; if you encourage him to do this he will allow you to express yourself more articulately and without this you won't feel heard or understood. The more you feel heard, the more you will be willing to give him the 'loving trust, acceptance, appreciation, admiration, approval, and encouragement that he needs' says relationship expert, John Gray.

If you ever feel hurt in a disagreement, try to forgive your husband, but always express your hurtfulness to him, or how would he know not to act in this manner again? In *Fascinating Womanhood* by Helen Andelin we are told to act as a spoilt child would if she was unhappy and didn't get what she wanted. She might pout, shake her curls and stamp her foot, all of which the husband might find endearing. Then again, he might not! I think what the author was trying to say here is that it's best to remain lighthearted and laugh about disagreements *whilst still expressing your feelings.* There is no reason why your husband would knowingly hurt you. So, if you let him know in a playful way, he won't take it as a criticism and put his defences up; he is more likely to respond than if you voice your concerns with anger or aggression. The funny thing is many women keep their feelings to themselves and literally have thoughts such as, he doesn't care because he hasn't asked me how I'm feeling/helped with the chores/bought me flowers this month (delete as necessary). But I need to tell you this, sisters—husbands are not mind readers! Help them out and tell him what you are thinking! And this brings us on nicely to the next topic.

6. Expressing Our Desires

Believe it or not, your husband's innermost desire is to make you happy. When he achieves this, he feels validated as a husband and even as a man. This innate desire to please you is 'alive and well' says Laura Doyle. It may not seem like it when there is a conflict and he responds with a defensive attitude but after this is over and he feels respected once again, 'he'll be looking for any chance to delight you.' When he knows what will make you happy, he will have the tools to feel successful as a husband.

When he uses these tools to make you happy, you're both happy. Don't forget that the mother usually has a stronger presence in the house and her mood usually affects everybody. That's why it's crucial to let your husband know what will make you happy. 'If mama's not happy, nobody's happy.' I actually believe the stability of a household lands on the shoulders of the wife and how she decides to tackle certain issues in her marriage and home. This is why it's important to always try to remain light-hearted. (I will discuss this further in Chapter Twelve).

One of my friends swears by the fact that the key to a successful marriage is being allowed a lie-in every Sunday! Her husband wants her to be happy. Happy Mama; Happy Household.

7. Hard Work

We expect the spouse who is working outside the home to work hard every day, to get up, not miss a day of work no matter how they're feeling (unless they're actually ill of course!) and generally do what they can to keep their job in order to bring back a wage packet every month.

In the same way, our work at home should be *worked at* and therefore, rather than just spending the day at home and whiling the time away, the spouse at home should try to be efficient, considerate and hard working. Unlike the spouse who works out of the house, we certainly don't get a monetary reward for our efforts. However, I see our reward as the *feeling of accomplishment when a job is complete,* which is actually part of good self-care. If both spouses are working outside the home, be prepared to work doubly hard inside the home. To bolster each other's ambitions, supporting each other so that any goals and desires are fulfilled in the best way is a fantastic way to show you care about your spouse. The Prophet ﷺ used to help out with household duties, but this sunnah has fallen down the wayside, particularly in South

Asian culture where the wife picks up the brunt of the house-work. If you're both working outside, try to share the workload inside the home more equally. Help each other out. Be a partner-ship. Work together to maintain a strong household.

It is important to mention here that one must be fully aware of the choices they have in a marriage and not to become a mar-tyr. Don't give so much of yourself that you lose yourself in the process. If you feel this way, the road to bitterness is nigh; pull yourself back and establish fair boundaries. Remember to keep the self-care and communication going, as that is key here to finding happiness and balance in your marriage.

8. Finding Time To Connect

ROUTINES

Having a rhythm and routine to your lives will really help to keep you sane, especially if you have a young family. This will in turn make your marriage less stressful and more likely to be full of beautiful moments. It's really important to have the chil-dren in bed on time (on weekdays, at least) thereby giving you time alone together. Maybe this doesn't work for you because of work commitments, etc. Maybe you just about have family time together when you sit and eat. That's great too. You'll find that when the routine is gone and you don't get that time together, you won't feel as 'connected'. It will be more difficult then to be in tune with one another's thoughts and feelings.

Although I do find that, in my family, if one of my children has had a late nap and is still around in the evening, neither of us is stressed and we find it easier to let the child nap than try to reason with a very ratty, tired child through the afternoon and early evening. I think it depends on how you, as a couple, handle this according to your preferences and tolerance levels.

DATE NIGHTS/WEEKENDS AWAY

It's really important to schedule time away with one another. If you have small children, consider leaving them with a close friend or relative for a night or even a weekend. It's so important to have a relationship outside the 'parenting' zone; it's a very special time for a mother to remember who she was before the time of nocturnal feeding and disturbed toilet breaks came about!

Again, in my family, this is a very rare occurrence as we've simply managed to find an equilibrium with the kids around on evenings out. We enjoy the lightheartedness children bring to the outing. If the kids are behaving in a difficult way outdoors, then we simply choose to spend family time indoors and enjoy a suitable activity together. Before we had kids of our own, we would regularly take out nieces and nephews for trips and would enjoy their individual quirks and innocent company, bless them. The message here is do what works for you as a family!

INTIMACY

To be open to intimacy (no matter how tired or disgusting you're feeling!) is so important. No matter whether we say a word or not, the pyjamas we wear, eye-contact (or lack of it!) and the differing bedtimes all speak volumes to our spouse. To be *open* to a kiss and a cuddle and maybe a massage to make you feel more connected will be like the helium needed to lift a relationship. This openness will mean that there will be no fear of rejection and therefore you are able to be more open with each other about other things too. Be honest about (and try to communicate!) your desires and needs here; the payoffs will speak for themselves! Try to keep things fresh in the bedroom, dress up for 'date nights', pencil certain dates in your diary and prepare in advance for it (doing this secretly would work beautifully). And also remember to be spontaneous too! Remember to remain 'open' even if it isn't the right day! Make your time special and important. You'll both be thankful for this connectedness once the children have grown and flown the nest. Your time invested now will mean you'll have a companion for life in the years to come inshaAllah!

Intimacy doesn't only translate to sexual intimacy, (although intimacy in the bedroom does lead to intimacy elsewhere), it also refers to a feeling of closeness and friendship that is second-to-none. When you nurture an environment of openness, honesty and love, the benefits are profound. You may even find that special soulmate you are seeking.

9. Love Languages

Neuro-Linguistic Programming (NLP) Practitioners have studied individuals and discovered that most people show love according to three distinct modalities. They categorised these distinctions into three languages of love: visual, audio, and kinesthetic. On the internet you'll also find gender-specific charts which will help you identify what language you and your spouse speak. Similarly, Gary Chapman named 5 Love Languages in his book and you can take a quiz to help you decide which ones best fit yours. See the Recommended Reading list at the end of the book for details on how to do this.

The idea behind these love languages is really profound and actually has the potential to change one's whole relationship. It certainly did mine. Once I found out my husband's Love Language was Acts of Service I completely understood why he hesitated to tell me how much he loved me but would wash up for me in a flash! Before I read about these languages I assumed he just didn't love me enough! (Sad times, I know). I want you to learn about these so that you can understood each other and become bilingual in the language of luurve!

So, in a nutshell, Chapman states there are 5 Love Languages. These are:

1. Words of affirmation
2. Acts of service
3. Receiving gifts
4. Quality time
5. Physical touch

If your spouse speaks a different language to yourself *you may not feel loved* and vice versa. It's so important to be aware of their Love Language so you show them love in a way that they understand and then they can also reciprocate.

10. Give Each Other Some Time and Space

Despite being intimately close, we should give our spouse their own space lest they feel suffocated by our love. 'Loving to death' may not cause one to die, but it can result in a very unhappy spouse who needs time to his/herself. We need to understand that although we are bound together as a couple, we are individuals. And the sooner we understand this human condition the happier we will be in our marriage. As Gibran, the 19th Century Lebanese-American poet, said:

'And sing and dance together and be joyous, but let each one of you be alone, even as the strings of a lute are alone though they quiver with the same music... stand together yet not too near together: For the pillars of the temple stand apart.'

And just like the pillars of a temple, both are required to stand upright and firm in order to do the job that was required of them. For a husband and wife to uphold a strong foundation and lofty structure overhead is to excel in the job of fulfilling the roles of heading a successful household.

I think it is natural for marriages to have ups and downs; to have moments of extreme bliss and harmony and then to experience days of indifference or even disappointment or disillusionment is totally expected. I think it's really important, in this instance, to begin each day afresh. Try to go to bed reconciled, if indeed there is substance in your lack of affection or synchronisation in thoughts or feelings. To endeavour to wake up to a new day will help you to get rid of any bad feelings. Keep any dregs of disappointment at bay and begin the day refreshed and with no grudges or regrets. Speak through anything that troubles you (see point 5). Rather than regret decisions, learn through mistakes that have been made instead—this is crucial for growth in relationships. Remember the phrase 'If only...' comes from the shaitaan. Try to look ahead. And of course, even a rainbow needs a bit of rain in order to shine brilliantly and become beautifully radiant.

May our marriages shine bright like a rainbow against our bright blue sky of life. As well as our marriages, there are other important relationships that need to be worked on in life. I will explore these in the next chapter.

Three Take-Home Points for Chapter Six

1. Seek help in a mentor, maybe an older person you respect, a book, or even a marriage course and strive to constantly work at it.
2. Communication is key.
3. Try not to keep a grudge overnight and endeavour to start every day afresh.

I totally believe that maintaining positive relationships ranks up there with healthy eating and exercise, which we will look at in Chapter Fourteen, as a necessary investment for your health. However, let's take a look at friendships first. One of the main positive effects of a good friendship is that it will boost your own happiness and reduce stress levels. If a friend of yours is happy, you're more likely to be, too. Friends usually cheer your successes and are encouraging and generous with their praise, therefore, they are handy to have about to improve your self-confidence and self-worth. This is not to say that they encourage arrogance but simply that they celebrate your good traits, which can be done hand-in-hand with praising Allah ﷻ, the Giver. You will also find help in coping with traumas, such as divorce, a serious illness, job loss or the death of a loved one in a good friendship.

Not only that, but friends model new ways of being and may inspire you to try something new and support your efforts to grow. With a good friend, you'll see your energy and creativity blossom.

They will also notice and try to help if they feel your life-style habits are getting in the way of living a good life. Within the bounds of a good friendship you are likely to encourage each other to stay away from what has been forbidden and you may also remind each other to establish good habits instead. The Prophet ﷺ said:

'A believer is a mirror of the believer.'
[Abu Dawud]

So what you see in your sisters in Islam is a reflection of what is within you. It helps to realign oneself if one is able to constantly check themselves with their friends, via an amiable close friendship.

We are a community-based religion, from jummah to gatherings of sacred knowledge, to reminders of the benefits of eating in groups. There are notable positive effects of being together, living together and praying together, alhamdulillah. People are known to be happier as they age, if they remain in positive relationships throughout their lives. Being socially engaged leads to more positive emotions, which in turn may actually boost your body's immune system and reduce the physical signs of stress.

Maintaining a friendship takes hard work and effort, but it's worth it! It's also important to be a good friend yourself, providing others with as many of the benefits of friendship as you can. It feels good to help others, and that only adds to your own happiness. Unfortunately most of us have suffered, at one time or another, from people that don't have a positive effect on our lives.

Beware of Toxic Friendships

OK, so, how do I know if I have a toxic friend?

If hanging out with them doesn't resonate with the true you and your aims and desires in life, then ask yourself these questions:

- Why am I friends with this person?
- Do I gain anything from this friendship?
- Am I giving anything of value into this relationship?

It's interesting to note how many people we have in our lives who are just there because we feel they have to be. Take them out of your life and you'll feel better for it. Negative friends just usurp your energy which can be used more effectively in a mutually giving and loving relationship.

A note on information-sharing

Be aware of giving too much information to anyone. Learn the art of being vague! When you give out too much information, it makes you vulnerable and there's no need for it. Keep your cards close to your chest—there is no need to spell out your next greatest venture or possible business idea. There's no need to be overly secretive either, because that's just weird! They'll find out in due course when the time is right, and this way, they won't have any 'ammunition' to bring you down next time they feel like it.

To further distinguish a toxic friendship from a healthy one, I have drawn up a table so that you can be clear on what you need to be aware of:

TOXIC FRIENDSHIP	HEALTHY FRIENDSHIP
They criticise you a LOT	They might help you to acknowledge your faults and lovingly suggest changes
They compare themselves to you and are competitive to an unhealthy degree that makes you feel uncomfortable	They may openly admire you but do not copy you excessively. You admire traits in them too and you learn from each other
They sometimes disregard your opinions	They listen to and appreciate your opinions
They sometimes ignore you completely in social situations	They value you and appreciate you, no matter who you're with
They make demeaning or petty remarks about you	They celebrate you as an individual
They make fun out of your ambitions and desires	They encourage and support you to live out your biggest dreams
They use secret past disclosures against you	They NEVER use information you have trusted them with against you
They have a negative impact on your deen and you don't look forward to spending time with them	They are usually a person of piety or filial goodness whom you love spending time with
They blame you for things that go wrong in their lives	They do not blame you for anything!

As I've got older, I've noticed that I am able to identify negative relationships more quickly. When I was younger I would always attribute my friends' 'weird behaviour' to myself, as I'm sure a lot of you do! You make excuses, you put it down to stress or a bad day or a certain situation and tell yourself that *you'll do better next time,* not realising that it's not you at all and that you're setting yourself up for a fall. Nowadays, I have less patience for these things. I really hope and pray that Allah ﷻ gives you great, positive healthy relationships in your life so you are easily able to identify and extricate yourself from the messy ones, inshaAllah.

The truth is, every negative relationship will not have everything mentioned in the boxes above, sometimes a person will only show one or two of these traits and honestly, I have found that I sometimes have to stay away from people who make me laugh or people who show me appreciation in other ways just so that I can look after myself and stay away from the negative effects of our friendship. It's not all black and white either as I've found that sometimes a relationship can be salvaged if you are able to talk things out. It could be that a misunderstanding or a presumption that one of you has about the other has made the relationship sour and that a renewal of understanding and love may be able to revive it BUT if you find that you are unable to turn things round, finish things up as fast as you can!

Practical tips to leave an unhealthy relationship

- My teacher's advice in this situation is to stop laughing at their jokes! People like to be appreciated so if you outwardly stop enjoying their company, they should soon get the message.
- Stop sharing information about your life with them.

- Make excuses so that you don't spend as much time together—when they ask to see you, explain that you're busy.
- Return their phone calls with a polite text message.
- If you find yourself sitting with them in a social situation, be polite but try to move to a 'safe' place as soon as you can.

I've noticed that these people are opportunists and will use any chance to exert their power over you, but once you've identified them as toxic, the effect on you and your psyche is diminished— you no longer have to wonder whether *you* said or did the wrong thing.

In fact, through identifying and steering clear of these relationships, you've done yourself a huge favour. Pat yourself on the back and remember to look out for these signs when making new friends. Good luck! Take care of yourself and may Allah ﷻ be with you.

Dealing With Conflict

A little note on family ties

We are taught the importance of keeping family relationships going, no matter what. Here is some advice on this topic.

Breaking family ties on purpose is not allowed. However, one *is* allowed to keep one's distance. Don't forget, Allah ﷻ is Just. There is no need to worry. Concentrate on the positive relationships in your life and try to have good manners with those relationships you struggle with. If there is a little animosity in the relationship, then soften the person's heart with a gift or two. A generous gift goes a long way, as does a random act of kindness.

There is an excellent example in our beloved Prophet ﷺ when he put up with the awful behaviour of the people around him through his good manners. This doesn't mean that you let people walk all over you, but that you interact with them in the best way that you can, and leave it at that. There is a fine line between letting things go and displaying patience, and in becoming a doormat. Look after yourself. Nothing in Islam says that you need to sacrifice your dignity and self-respect in order to maintain a family relationship. Make a decision to keep your distance. Self-preservation is a thing. And it's important. Something to think about. The friends you choose to spend time with say a lot about you too.

It is a very sad thing that those we love the most have the ability to hurt us like nobody else. When there is a disagreement, when things get heated and words have been said that one regrets, it's really important to hold on to the idea to 'let it all go'.

To have perfect memories of how people we love have let us down will never work for us and will, in fact, inhibit the chance of true happiness in this universe. When your memory doesn't serve you well in times of conflict, this is a very good thing! To forget how you have been wronged in the past is, in fact, a gift.

I've already spoken about the negative influence some friends (and family) have in life and how it's so important to set boundaries and not allow these people to take centre stage. Now you must remember to keep this in mind when deciding whether any relationship is worth salvaging.

When things go wrong ask yourself: Does this relationship add value to my life? Is any negativity overwhelmingly outweighed by the positive impact it has?

If the answer is yes, yes, a million times over yes, then you know you have a relationship worth fighting for. This person needs to be told, in no uncertain terms, that you are sorry and regret what has been said. If you've been hurt, try your best to forgive and forget, in order to move forward.

1. You may have to take a stance to resolve some issues.

Talk things out; write things down if you need to. Think about topics that you should steer away from in the future. I remember my parents' advice about not ever arguing about money or family matters. If this advice was heeded at all times, I can just imagine the conflict that would have been avoided! Be honest with each other.

If you find that the same topic keeps coming up again and again, make a resolution to:

a. Stop bringing it up
b. Deal with the reason why it's such a volatile issue (ask yourself what your own personal issues are with this topic)
c. Try to come to a mutual understanding or compromise which means that you'll both deal with it better in the future.

2. The second way which will help you move forward is to stay quiet!

Use masking tape (or duct tape) if you have to but keep your mouth closed. It will avoid so many future battles! Two quotes come to mind here:

> *'If duct tape doesn't work, you're not using enough!'*
> [Anon]

Our Beloved Messenger of Allah ﷺ said:

> *'Speak good or remain silent.'*

Silence is golden. Silence is also underrated. Indeed, the other benefits of silence are many. See Chapter Fifteen for more on this.

I was once given the priceless advice that when in a conflict, one must never say 'the worst thing ever'. It's the nastiest thing you could say about a person. This 'thing' could be the 'Achilles' heel' of a person; a weakness, a vulnerability that generally only the people closest to that person know about. If it is ever uttered, it will be so, so difficult to backtrack and take it back. Equally, it will be very difficult for the other person to take it out of their mind in order to forgive and forget.

This piece of advice is golden. Take heed and don't ever utter those words.

To forgive and forget as quickly as you can is wonderful if you can do it, and also healing. If you can learn to take a slice of humble pie and do this, it is so rewarding—you'll be able to salvage even the most tenuous of relationships.

In an argument with one's spouse, one of my teachers advises people to say:

YOU ARE RIGHT
IT'S ALL MY FAULT
I AM SORRY!

99.9% of the time this works like the *shifa* of all arguments!

Use variations. Change it around a bit. But ultimately, using these three sentences is the saviour of all relationships. It actually deflates a potentially large, previously unresolvable conflict. It opens the doors for forgiveness each time, for what has been upset but our egos (nafs) through all of this?

When we admit that it is our fault (afterwards you can clarify and accept only partial blame! It takes two after all, haha), it acts as an extinguisher for the ego. With the ego subdued, there is nowhere for the argument to go and it often fizzles out. Skeptical? Try it and see!

Once the situation (read rage) has been diffused somewhat, it's easier at that point to get to the crux of the matter:

Why do you feel so hurt?

How can we ensure that this doesn't happen again?

If it's a spouse issue—because let's face it, we all have those—then my mum has always advised me to 'carry on as normal' when it comes to serving the family and fulfilling my duty in the household (whether it's going to work in the morning or carrying out the school run or any other duty which pertains to managing the household). Yes, there has to be a consequence if you're not happy but there's no need to involve other family members in your disagreement!

I've noticed that this really does stop a situation from escalating. It's a message that everything will be fine; it's reassuring and full of love. It ensures love will indeed prevail, after all this has passed. It helps in changing the conflict from boiling rage to simmering tempers and puts a lid on any substance that may have taken form had these responsibilities or duties been neglected.

A couple of notes on Silent Treatment:

- Husbands usually enjoy this 'time out'!
- 'Ladies, Stop Doing What Doesn't Work!'

When I was younger, I used to use this 'strategy' to deal with situations I wasn't happy with. As I got older, I noticed how it just prolonged matters and didn't give me what I needed to get over the situation; in fact, it was literally prolonging my feeling of hurt. I felt misunderstood and hurt for longer. Silent treatment is actually 'a psychic communication strategy to punish people for not properly reading our minds'.

It's ridiculous really. The best way to deal with things like this is open communication. Speak about the issue! Try to resolve it in the best of manners, when all is calm.

And if you are ever at the receiving end of silent treatment, go and do something you love or indulge in a bit of self-care and don't worry about it. If something needs changing, it'll come to you without you brooding over it or worrying about your own self-worth. And if the other person needs time to cool down, you can give them that without feeling too bad about it. Communication is key here.

Once again, here is a reminder that to talk over an issue and be open about the situation is the best way forward. I think the main thing is to try to come to an agreement, in the most amicable way you can and then try your best to stick to it.

Remember the 5 love languages?

To know the love language of the person you're in a conflict with is so important. An example of what can go wrong if you don't know about this is as follows:

I was having a discussion with a close friend and in the middle I got up and hugged her. She said to me she didn't want fake hugs; she wanted to be heard. I concluded that her love language must be the gift of quality time and words of affirmation. By hugging her, she actually felt like I wasn't listening and therefore felt unloved! I didn't mean to upset her at all, but I did so unknowingly and it was so shocking! With a start I remembered the Love Languages, gave a little nod to Gary Chapman, and tried to listen as open-heartedly as I could. It worked wonders.

Once the correct Love Language is known, it's much easier to make amends. Even the mere decision to make amends is a huge step in the right direction and the barakah (blessings) of this should help shape the next few steps in making amends and for your relationship to be full of light, love, the possibility of forgiveness and new beginnings inshaAllah.

Dr. Gary Chapman said that we need to be aware of reacting automatically to a situation, without allowing ourselves to think about things before we speak. If we let our instincts take over and speak in a defensive manner, we are likely to offend the person we love and it will be really unhealthy for our relationship. If, on the other hand, we take our time to respond during a volatile situation, we will be more likely to engage in a 'calmer, more productive conversation' which is much healthier for the overall relationship.

When the other person isn't ready to receive your apologies or attempts at resolving the situation, it is definitely a sign to quieten down. Swallow your ego and let the other person get the last word in. Pacify their ego until the person has calmed down enough to talk. Overall, it won't change the consequence of your disagreement. Just know that this isn't a fruitful time for this discussion.

Time is a great healer in matters such as this and hopefully you will be able to go over things in a calmer and more appropriate manner after some time has lapsed, and you are able to gain some perspective. The Prophet ﷺ said:

> 'The example of good company is like being in a perfumery, either remnants of the perfume remain on you or you will carry the perfume in your hands; and the example of bad company is like visiting the establishment of the blacksmith, where you will either be affected by the smoke or you will carry the scent of it!'

This is a reminder of how much the people around you affect you, whether there is consent or not! Similarly, the motivational speaker Jim Rohn famously said that:

*'We are the average of the five people we spend the
most time with.'*

No matter how much we want to be individuals and choose our own way, the people we hang around with the most will definitely influence us (whether we like it or not). That's why it's important to remember the choices we have in life and always try to be mindful who we choose to spend our quality time with.

Lastly, a note about company vs loneliness. The Prophet ﷺ once said:

*'Loneliness is better than bad company, and good
company is better than being alone.'*

A reminder here to be mindful of the friends we make, realising that good company can be the making of you. Not only that, but we must also remember that loneliness is better than hanging out with the wrong crowd. This speaks volumes in terms of getting together with good friends regularly, and keeping away from those who have a bad influence on you. When thinking about peer pressure and bad company we tend to emphasise the problem within teens and younger ladies, but older ladies can also be influenced by certain crowds of friends. Be aware of those friendship circles that tend to gossip and talk about people when they are not present. It is OK to talk about situations and people if you are seeking nasiha but other than that, avoid such talk. You will be better off for it! A word to the wise—when people can openly discuss others in front of you, who says they are not talking about you to others? I wouldn't trust them with my friendship as far as I can throw them! Be careful, ladies. Stick to the discussion of the good and the true, and inshaAllah you can't go wrong.

And there we have it. A few thoughts on maintaining positive relationships. If you are sitting on your own and reading this, go ahead and put the book down. Send a message to your friend, or group of friends. Send them a hug emoji and let them know you are thankful for all the reasons above and indulge in the warm fuzzy feeling it gives you. Send a thankful prayer upwards in gratitude for the wonderful friends and family in your life. Alhamdulillah!

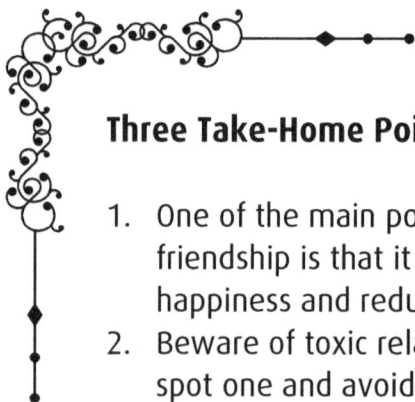

Three Take-Home Points for Chapter Seven

1. One of the main positive effects of a good friendship is that it will boost your own happiness and reduce stress levels.
2. Beware of toxic relationships. Know how to spot one and avoid it at all costs.
3. A huge help in avoiding conflicts is to keep one's own mouth shut—somebody cannot continue an argument on their own and it's highly entertaining to watch them stomp their feet in frustration because you have chosen not to comply and lose your cool. Trust me, you'll love it!.

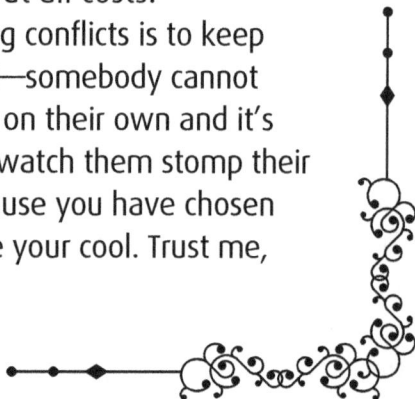

Next, I will write about the thorny topic of bringing up children in the West. Wish me luck!

Chapter Eight
Bringing Up Children in the West

I was very hesitant to write this chapter because I am so aware that ideas on parenthood cover a huge spectrum. Parenthood is wrought with reactions to circumstances and making the best of the situation you have at hand, and it is a subjective topic. Even though I have five children alhamdulillah, I am still learning and I will be the first to say that the advice I have laid out in this chapter can be improved upon.

My husband and I had an intention to 'do something different' with our children and to help them through childhood with a clear focus. That is to live a good, fulfilling life which focuses on Islam from a young age, to build good character through example and to keep good company.

We decided to home educate our first child and then subsequently our second and third until I was pregnant with my fourth child. As I mentioned earlier, at this point I decided it was too much and after much deliberation and consideration we put all three children into a local Steiner School.

A quick note on Steiner education

Steiner education is based on the educational philosophy of Rudolf Steiner, an Austrian philosopher and social reformer. Its pedagogy strives to develop pupils' intellectual, artistic, and practical skills in an integrated and holistic manner. The cultivation of pupils' imagination and creativity is a central focus. Children do not learn to read and write in a formal manner until the age of (at least) 6 or 7 at which time they are in Class One. Prior to this most of their education consists of learning through play and imitation of the home environment through cooking, cleaning, laundry, gardening, baking, water and sand play, etc.

We were very blessed to find an open and welcoming community in the West Midlands and I feel that my children benefited from the creative curriculum, the wholesome holistic lifestyle (which encouraged long-term sustainable choices for our planet in the choices we make for ourselves including the food we ate) and in asserting the children with a self-belief like no other. To use a phrase coined in a book (recommended to me by a very wise and pious friend) by Wayne Dyers called *What Do We Really Want For Our Children?*, I had learnt, through Steiner education, to teach my children how to become 'limitless' human beings.

Thus, I spent a total of four years home educating (plus about six months when we moved to Leicester later on in life) and about two and a half years as a Steiner mum. From this experience I gleaned that you could do worse than to adhere to the following advice for those of you who are thinking about (or already involved in) home education. Indeed, you could follow a few of these points to supplement a state school education too! I am going to refrain from analysing Steiner education—suffice to say it's not perfect but it worked for us at the time of our lives when we needed it... If it is something you are considering, please take your time to visit it and make the most of any trial period they may offer. Make istikhara, as I'm sure you will do anyway and then follow your instinct. If it's a good fit for your child(ren) and your family, go for it. May Allah ﷻ be with you!

And now to tips on home education:

- Join a weekly Forest School Session. The wonder and awe from learning about nature whilst spending regular quality time outdoors together is second-to-none. I have recently trained as a forest school practitioner myself and am now an even bigger advocate for outdoor learning. The scope for learning on a holistic level and the effect on mental health is astounding. I am so excited about the new initiatives which are bringing forest school experiences to the average state school child.

- Take part in other wider community events. There are many active Facebook pages and online groups that meet regularly; these are vital if you are to remain sane over these years. Other home educators and their families will become your tribe. They're the only people who will understand why you would ever decide to take on this mammoth task willingly! Note: Try not to pack too much into your week. Get the children used to down-time at home too. Three or four morning/afternoon sessions are plenty to be getting on with. This way you won't tire yourself out and can establish a good home routine inshaAllah.

- Remember that you don't have to stick to a rigid timetable! Do what suits you. If your spouse has days off work for one reason or another go for family trips out during term time. Take advantage of quiet flights and tickets abroad outside of the usual holiday periods.

- Read read read! Surround yourselves with books; books from the library, books at home, novels, reference books, magazines, audiobooks and read aloud to the children whenever you get a chance. Not only are you creating beautiful memories whilst planting a lasting love of learning new things, you'll also be able to relax and unwind together knowing that the education is taking care of itself.

- Buy lots of random arts and craft resources—coloured paper, glue, coloured pencils, paint, etc. These will come in handy for DIY craft sessions that your child will become independent in learning with. Learn to upcycle, reusing a lot of materials in the house that others would recycle.

- Do involve the children with the household chores and the general upkeep of the house. This way you can keep up with everything and not have to feel guilty about not spending time with the kids. Sorting clothes, polishing windows and doors, sweeping, tidying, washing dishes, cooking, baking and even planning and shopping for dinner are all fantastic ways to get the children to learn about real life, not to mention easing your job role too!

- Play to your strengths. If you're musical, consider singing or learning how to play an instrument together. If you're into baking or cooking, spend lots of time in the kitchen together. Your children will become proficient at adult activities if you let them. My daughter was baking bread at four years old, to the point of getting out all the correct ingredients and beginning to measure them out all by herself. My sons learnt how to play the duff (a frame drum) from a young age simply because I used to go to weekly singing sessions myself and dragged the children along with me.

- Pair up with another family (or two) and swap your children to teach different subjects. Not only do you get a break but everybody involved will find it refreshing to work with somebody different for a little while (not to mention other people's children are better listeners!). I did this twice during my home schooling journey and still remember each family we paired up with so fondly. A bond is created through learning and journeying through life together, and I felt that the load and responsibility was also shared, making it a fantastic experience for all.

- Always, always make time for yourself. Yes, it's that all-important topic of self-care again. I feel that I should have done this a lot more. I thought too much about what people thought of me. I took comments personally and let them affect what I was doing. If I was able to give my young self some advice I would say: Well done! You're doing a great job and you will continue doing so even if you send your kids to school. Home education does not need six hours a day of doing school-y things; on the contrary, one-on-one tuition is much more concise and effective. Quality presides over quantity when comparing with the school system.

Even though, as a teacher, I was aware of the fact that one-hour of quality one-to-one tuition could achieve the same results as a whole week at school on the same subject, I'd still allow myself to be swayed by one person's opinion or another. If you decide to put your own needs first—your sanity and strength and peace of mind—it does not make you a bad parent, or indeed it shouldn't make you think that you failed! I felt that I gave out too much information to too many people and then ended up having to justify my decisions, rather than keeping the decisions made within the bounds of close family and getting on with things quietly. This keeping up with expectations encroached on my self-care time. By telling my young self to not care about other people's opinions, I would do what needed to be done and at the same time make sure that I took regular time out for my own needs without the extra guilt.

- Establish a daily 'quiet time' which consists of an afternoon nap time for the youngest and quiet reading time for the older ones.
- We all know that the children can continue to learn no matter what time or day it is but, for the sake of your own sanity, don't make every single experience a learning one. You'll tire yourself out. Give yourself a break and have a cut-off point. I used to stop at around 3pm. After this I used to prioritise the family dinner (without little hands in the kitchen!), and stopped being 'teacher' for the day. It took me a while to establish but once I did, it was a huge relief.

So there we have it, a quick guide to home education. I wish you all the best on your home education journey. Above all, remember to have fun!

The second topic I wish to discuss is discipline. We began with a very soft approach with my first child, and only realised how spoilt she was when, at two years old, she had a new baby brother and we had to deal with her temper tantrums. She wouldn't listen to what I said and would embarrass me in public by her unruly behaviour. I began to use Time Out (using a number of minutes according to how old she was at the time). I'd say that was quite effective and I still use it now (thankfully, not so much with my eldest!). The main challenge when the children are younger is remaining consistent, as sometimes the younger siblings will take your attention away from dealing with the situation at hand appropriately.

I found that as my first three children were growing up they tended to get what they wanted because I'd give in simply to avoid a tantrum. I then learnt that as the adult in the situation I had the right to get what I wanted and had to learn not to back down so easily.

I'll give you an example. Children are very clever. They know when time is short or when they are being observed. They use this information to get what they want and can actually be very manipulative in this way! What I learnt was I had to stand my ground. I had to be firm and clear and not back down until I got what I wanted. Now I wasn't totally inflexible in this regard as I wouldn't usually use this approach in public. If I realised we weren't getting anywhere I would back down in that instance, only to vow that the child in question would be deprived of a treat (or something) in order for there to be a consequence for this misbehaviour later on. This seemed to work really well. I knew that if this happened it was an indication that the child needed 'retraining' in this area once we were back at home.

'Retraining' in this instance means role play undertaken at home so that the expectations required are clear from the out-set. In a nutshell, discipline in this regard is all about repetition and clear instructions.

Teachers actually use this method in Primary Education and it can be very effective. For example, if we were going to a friend's house I would sit the children down in a row on the sofa beforehand and put a plate of food out in front of them. I would model speaking politely, eating with good manners, not leaving the room the host had put us in and not nosing about looking into every cupboard and drawer in the room.

The book *Islamic Manners* by Shaykh Abdal-Fattah Abu Ghud-dah is an absolute treasure to read and helps so much with im-plementing good manners with your children.

In a time when toddlers enter areas of a host's house in the name of 'exploration' and 'learning', it is very valuable (even for adults) to learn and understand that even though in Islam a guest can stay for three days without prior notice, the host also has rights over his guest—one of them being that we must stay in the room we are put in and respect his or her privacy at all times.

As the kids grew older I learnt about spending quality time with each child. More often than not, when a child plays up it is a cry for attention. If we stop what we are doing and try to give time to that particular child (or even better, anticipate a problem and nip it in the bud by acting fast) we usually find that the problem dissipates quickly and easily. One of the things that is fascinating about children (even teens) is that they're not fully formed yet! They are still learning, they make bad decisions and we need to remember this and give them that leeway to make mistakes. We have to try to remain uncritical and show them unconditional love no matter what. We have to forgive them and give them a chance to correct themselves without anger or humiliation. It is crucial to remember that each stage they go through is temporary and to not be overly sensitive to the way we are treated by them.

Role play is useful in how to respond to particular complaints and how to question and comment on what children say to us without shutting them down. This approach is outlined in Faber and Mazlish's *How to Talk So Kids Will Listen & Listen So Kids Will Talk*. When learning to value a child's opinion, I was struck by how it resonated with the Prophetic example of giving a person (a child or otherwise) one's full attention. I would say that even though a lot of the advice given in this book is prevalent in lots of child-centred psychology books that came after it (it was written in 1982), I still found it a refreshing read as it served as a reminder that children (however selfish and spoilt they may seem), behave according to their own rational logic and talking to them can get to the bottom of any disappointing behavioural patterns. Three really important things I gleaned from this book were:

1. To prioritise one-on-one quality time with each child, with the intention of improving overall communication. For example, doing things like cooking and baking together is a wonderful way of increasing the bond with your children.
2. To take a long-term approach to parenting. To not worry about the here and now and to avoid thinking each phase will last forever.
3. To utilise people around you as positive role models. Teenagers often feel they can talk to other grown-ups more easily than their own parents.

Another book I have recently read that I recommend is *The Book You Wish Your Parents Had Read (and Your Children Will Be Glad That You Did)* by Phillipa Perry. I like the way the author focuses on a parent's own upbringing and how it may affect their parenting skills. She also emphasises the fact that we have to simply accept that we will make mistakes and helps us decide what to do about them. A very interesting read. At the moment, one of the gems from the book I have found very pertinent is the use of a 'love bomb'. It's especially useful when one of your children feels neglected and needs some one-on-one attention in order to reset their love gauge. It involves a set amount of quality time that you spend with one of your children—the fact that this time is with one child at a time is one of the main factors—and you ask them how to spend it. The author speaks about spending time out of the home and doing anything with them within sensible limits. However, I recommend doing this at whatever level is easy for you at the time. For example, an hour or two when the other children are out or asleep works really well. You could cook dinner or bake desserts together and even watch something together. The fact that you're putting them first will really boost their happiness and fill their love tanks inshaAllah.

These parenting approaches have given me many strategies to deal with the many obstacles that we've come across over the last decade and more as our children have been growing up.

Over the years, I've learnt that parenting is a huge project, one that cannot be taken lightly. If you are worried about the way your children are behaving as they are growing up, try to seek help from parents you admire, either in your family or in the general community. As I've mentioned before, we as an *ummah* are very social. We are told to keep family ties, give salaams to each other, to study together and also pray together when we can. Seeing people regularly and seeking advice is also excellent to help us manage stressful situations in life.

Don't ever feel like you're alone in this. We all have our bad days. Nobody is perfect at this difficult job. The children will go through phases and you, as their mother, have only got to do your best. After that, pray your hardest that they will turn out to be righteous human beings. They are an *amanah* given to us and they have a right to be brought up in a fair manner. This is something we should be aware of. Do what you think is right instinctively and always ask Allah ﷻ to help.

This is an all-encompassing, beautiful dua for our children which has been repeated often by parents whose children I have admired. SubhanAllah, the sincere dua of a mother does wonders.

> *'Our Lord! Grant unto us wives and offspring who will
> be the comfort of our eyes, and give us (the grace) to
> lead the righteous.'*
> [Quran 25:74]

Tarbiya-wise I've seen that an Islamic primary school is amazing in helping children form an identity and a strong bond with the deen. Children are also usually able to pray together and this helps them to establish a connection with their Creator. It is our job, after that, to help them maintain this bond.

We have to remember that our children will not be perfect; indeed, we are not ourselves perfect so we shouldn't be surprised! In fact, they will excel in different areas—those who are night owls may be excellent at *Qiyam al-Layl* and those who don't like eating much will not find fasting a chore, etc. We have to help them play to their strengths, and as I've written in previous chapters, if we allow them to do what they love as they are growing up, they will enjoy success inshaAllah.

Our own character as parents plays a huge part in shaping the child. Rather than always telling your child what to do, show them what is expected of them with your own good actions. How will they learn to be truthful or to not backbite if they see grown-ups around them doing the same thing? Actions speak louder than words. The best thing we can do is try our utmost to show them a good example.

Try to keep communication open. I read recently that parents should try to stay in touch with their own childlike nature—laughing, playing, being creative and also lighthearted will all help in making oneself more approachable to your children. Some parents even adopt their children's lingo (much to the children's consternation!) and this helps bridge the gap and improve communication for all. It means they'll always feel heard.

Quality family time is crucial. Simple things like eating together as much as you can in the week helps to strengthen bonds. In this day and age, a reminder is probably needed to limit screen time to improve communication. We will probably be thankful for apps like WhatsApp when they have left the family home but while they are within a few feet, these apps only increase the distance! Try to adopt screen-free family time at least once in the day. Use this time to catch up, to fulfil household duties together and use the quiet time to connect. Whether you're in silence or not, there will be benefit in working together closely without distractions.

That's all. All I can say now is to remind you to do your best, be sincere and ask Allah ﷻ for help. May Allah be with you. May we all find success in helping our children find a beautiful way of communicating and living in harmony together inshaAllah.

Three Take-Home Points for Chapter Eight

1. Rather than always telling your child what to do, show them what is expected of them with your own good actions. Actions speak louder than words.
2. Read through the tips on home schooling, knowing every educational journey is different. I pray that Allah ﷻ guides us to do what's best for our children at all times.
3. Quality time with your child is crucial and precious. It means that your child will have a healthy model to implement when he or she is ready to begin preparing for their own household one day.

The next topic I will discuss is living through the great detriment of the loss of a loved one. May Allah help us through such hardship with ease, contentment and understanding.

Chapter Nine
Losing Loved Ones

Given the fact that I have lost no less than five close family members in the last two years, it is no surprise that a chapter in this book is devoted to the subject of death and how to deal with the loss of loved ones.

Our beloved Prophet ﷺ said:

'The most intelligent person is the one who remembers death often.'

Those of us who have experienced the death of a close family member may describe it as a wake-up call of the greatest kind. I think it is both shocking and a huge miracle to have a living, walking, talking person simply cease to exist one day. It is earth-shattering, life-altering and a huge reminder that this life is temporary. It seems as though just as things are starting to work out in this duniya, we are brought back to questioning why we are actually here. We are given a massive reminder that life doesn't end here; we are reminded to be patient as life is a test, and we have to make the most of the time we have here on earth to accumulate good deeds and do our best in terms of serving people and perfecting our servitude before Allah ﷻ.

I really feel that one of the biggest blessings of having faith in the afterlife is the hope that one feels in being reunited with one's beloved lost relatives in Paradise. We have a great hope in being able to pray for them (subhanAllah we are so blessed that any good deeds performed in their name will benefit them as well as us) and ultimately, being reunited with them in the hereafter inshaAllah.

In believing that Allah ﷻ is Just, we are comforted in the knowledge that our deceased relatives' lives were never lived in vain. There is and always will be wisdom behind every act and every event that the passed soul had to endure, even if we don't know it at the time. The solace we receive from the reflection that this life is but a few minutes on this earth in comparison to an eternal life in the hereafter, helps hugely in acceptance of destiny and in being content with what we have here on earth. After all, life in this duniya has one huge undeniable reality—not one of us will get out alive! SubhanAllah. Let's make the most of our time, before it is over.

'But you prefer the worldly life, while the Hereafter is
better and more enduring.'
[Quran 87:16-17]

'What is this world but a dream that a sleeper sees; He
delights in it for a few moments, and then wakes up to
face reality.'
[Hassan Al-Basri]

'And this life of the world is only amusement and play!
Verily, the home of the Hereafter is the real life.
If only they knew.'
[Quran 29:64]

The fact is that when somebody dies not only should it affect us emotionally but also physically. It should shake us into action; into a stronger belief that this life is only temporary and of the great truth of our own mortality. Our shared grief and tears not only bind us remaining family members, but also release a much-needed anguish from the heart, reminding us that we are not alone and we still have each other.

We, who are left here on earth, can do a great service by remembering and praying for our loved ones whenever we raise our hands in supplication.

When asked how one can benefit their parents once they have passed away, the Prophet ﷺ replied:

> *'There are four things: praying and asking forgiveness for them, carrying out their promises, being good to their friends, and giving proper attention to those kinship bonds which could have only been attended to by them.'*

He ﷺ also said:

> *'Were it not for the living the dead would have been doomed.'*

In other words, the prayers and requests for forgiveness and mercy which they receive greatly benefit them in the next life.

One of the greatest things that one may offer to the dead is to recite the Quran and send on the reward for it. This is of great benefit and barakah. Muslims have agreed on this everywhere throughout the ages, the majority of scholars and virtuous people have recommended it, and there are ahadith to confirm this. Although, these ahadith have weak chains of transmission, there is a principle, as the hadith scholar al-Suyuti (may God show him His mercy) has said, that: 'Weak ahadith may be acted upon when they indicate acts of goodness. And these are indeed acts of goodness.'

This is so beautiful. I can't begin to say how much peace one feels when reciting the Quran for someone who has passed away. We are told the person will receive the Quran one recites as a beautifully wrapped gift. The heart is peaceful, reciting the melodious and soothing tones of the Quran and it is gladdened in the knowledge that it will ease the burden of their deceased relative.

Once the grieving period is over, we are told to once again renew our faith and practice with a greater zeal; knowing we haven't got long to live ourselves, until we, too, are taken away from this earth. We are told to:

> 'Make the most of five before five: one's youth before old age, one's health before ill health, one's free time before being busied, one's wealth before poverty, and one's life before death.'

Anyone who has attained any of these five and then lost them will tell you that they wished they had made the most of the time before it had come upon them.

We are told to visit the graveside often, as the believer in the grave is informed that we are there and can hear everything we say. In this regard, graveyards are an extension of the gardens of peace which lay beyond. The Prophet ﷺ said:

> 'No man visits the grave of his brother and sits by it but that he (the dead man) finds solace in this, having his spirit restored to him until the visitor departs.'

*'A dead (person) in his grave is never more
comforted than when those that he loved
in the world pay him a visit.'*

I have witnessed my own peace of mind and solace after
missing a loved one and then visiting their grave. I'm sure many
people agree with me that the visiting of a graveside brings
great peace to the heart and it is a huge blessing if one lives near
the graveside of their deceased relative and is able to visit often.

And now we turn to the topic of addressing the death of a
loved member of the family or a close friend through a fatal illness, for example, cancer. For surely, once or twice in our lives,
given the statistics, we are likely to hear about a loved one being
diagnosed with this awful disease. It is the most difficult news
to bear and yet we are told that to know that one's departure is
imminent is truly a blessing; indeed who knows how long any
one of us have got in this temporary world? The first thing we
are taught to say when we hear of a calamity is the soothing
ayah of the Quran:

$$(إِنَّا لِلَّهِ وَإِنَّا إِلَيْهِ رَاجِعُونَ)$$

'Indeed, to Allah we belong and to Him we shall return.'
[Quran 2:156]

It is a reminder that nothing on this earth belongs to us. We
have all come from Allah ﷻ and will return to Him. The best
we can do is to make the most of this borrowed time we have
on earth. It is a reminder to the one who is ill and those around
them to take heed of the message that we haven't got long on
this earth. The doctors don't know a lot about the causes and
effects of this disease and they estimate how long a person has

got left on this earth according to what they do know. However, we know that even though they are ill, it is not a guarantee that they will go first.

If you have heard that someone you love has recently been diagnosed with this disease, it will help to increase one's acts of worship and to maintain closeness to Allah ﷻ yourself. You will find a certain peace and acceptance simply through a renewed closeness inshaAllah. Secondly, make yourself available to that person, let them know you are thinking of them and are there to help or talk if they need to. Cancer is a disease of the mind as much as a disease of the body and it will be important for you to try to keep the person's spirits up as much as possible. Thirdly, don't despair. Allah in His Infinite Wisdom has decreed a matter and He knows best why this has happened. Have faith that every single one of us is being looked after by our loving Creator and know that whatever happens, if we have true faith in Allah, He will grant us patience and wisdom to help us through. It is helpful to look at other highly influential and inspiring people who have survived tests such as these. Let's look at one such person now.

There was once a young man named Ali Banat, who was a truly inspirational soul and you will soon discover why. In 2018, he died aged thirty-two, from cancer. His message resonated with a lot of people because he was so young, yet so full of acceptance with his condition. When he was first diagnosed, he was given only seven months to live and then he went on to live three more years. Four months after he was diagnosed he made a video called *'Gifted With Cancer'* which went viral. In the video, you get an idea of his lavish lifestyle and his spending habits.

Ali's reaction to his diagnosis was admitting that all the material wealth he possessed meant nothing to him and that in actual fact he had decided to give it all away. He was a millionaire and had accumulated lots of designer clothing, watches and jewellery. When Ali showed off his £450,000 Ferrari Spider in the video, he said: 'When you find out you're sick or you don't have much time to live, this is the last thing you want to chase' and 'It will change our perspective and help us to realign our priorities.'

Following his diagnosis, he launched a charity project called 'Muslims Around the World'. He emphasised how his priorities had shifted to doing good deeds and looking after his akhira. To give to charity is a huge blessing for those fortunate enough to be able to do it. Indeed, it has been reported that it is not necessarily only the rich who give to charity; in fact, poorer people actually give more. Maybe they have less to lose, but it's a great reminder that we don't have to be rolling in money in order to dig deep and give to those less fortunate than ourselves. InshaAllah it will purify our wealth, put barakah in it and it will actually make us feel richer if we do so.

Since his death (may Allah ﷻ grant him the highest place in Paradise), his story and message has been reported in various national and local newspapers around the world.

It is a reminder of the good we can do whilst here on earth; the legacy of goodness and hope that we can leave behind. It is proven that such acts of goodness will actually lengthen our lives. Rather than being bogged down with the thought that he wouldn't have much longer on this earth, his mindset changed to making the best of the time he had left. We have a lot to learn from this. If only we would realise that our days are also numbered.

His is a message of hope and love and commitment to Allah ﷻ and our purpose here on earth. Ali decided to realign his thoughts and desired to try to become the best human being that he possibly could and by doing so, he set a great example for us all, may Allah, the Most High, bless him.

Now, what can we do but ask for a beautiful ending? And pray that Allah ﷻ gives us a goodly life? Let's make an intention now, to live our best life, for the sake of Allah and His Beloved Last Messenger ﷺ.

In the book *Joy Jots* by Tamara Gray, which was gifted to me by one of my dearest friends (and is a book which I highly recommend!), we are reminded to do our utmost to make the most of our lives before it ends. The author reminds us that if we wish to have a *husnal-khatim* (an ending that is good), we must strive to complete our projects. We must remain optimistic and enthusiastic and keep our eye on the final goal.

She tells us that her theory is that 'if we work hard to create husnal-khitam in our daily lives, Allah ﷻ will bless us with it at the end of our lives.' InshaAllah!

May He, with His beautiful Love and Mercy shower us with blessings and an ease and comfort in knowing that this life is not all there is; that we will meet our loved ones in the next life and in the most beautiful of manners. May He make us of those who are content in knowing we can benefit them as we are still here on this earth. May our hearts be gladdened by this news. May He help us to make the most of our time on this earth!

I hope reading this has helped you as much as researching about this has helped me. May God bless you. May He make easy all your losses in this life. Ameen.

Three Take-Home Points for Chapter Nine

1. Death of a loved one should shake us into action, into a stronger belief that this life is only temporary and of the great truth of our own mortality.

2. Ali Banat's story is a reminder of the good we can do whilst here on earth; the legacy of goodness and hope that we can leave behind.

3. Through life-changing events, we need to accept that our days are also numbered and that we must be mindful of what we achieve in this life, so that we can make the most of it.

PART THREE

Let's now shift the topic from our loved ones to ourselves. How should we look after ourselves in the best way? Is self-care self-indulgent or crucial to our survival and sanity? Read the next chapter to find out! I am here to remind you that there are many aspects of self-care that can be introduced in your life. If you can't think of any right now, I've even written you a list(!). This final part of the book explores the many ways we can look after ourselves so that we are always presenting our best selves to society and more crucially, in general, we are the ones who will benefit from such a perspective at the end of the day.

Time management is a hot topic at the moment, and the ticking clock is something we are reminded of in our Holy Book too.

'By time. Verily, mankind is in loss. Except for those who have believed and do righteous deeds and advise each other to truth and advise each other to patience.'
[Quran 110:1-3]

In this chapter I include many tips to help you make the most of your time here on this precious earth. And whenever I need a reminder too, this is the list I peruse! I go on to discuss stress management tips including a reminder to not take life too seriously and to remain lighthearted even when things go a bit pear-shaped. I think it is so important to tame the inner-critic in us, for who says we always have to be perfect? This duniya is full of imperfections and there are many times when we simply do not get things right. The sooner we accept this and are able to laugh at ourselves, the easier it will be.

I spend a chapter discussing the importance of limiting wi-fi and social media in the home; I include the detrimental effects it has on us and what we can do to lessen the harm. I go on to address healthy eating and exercise, sleep and stillness and being content. I think these topics go hand-in-hand in helping to maintain a healthy lifestyle inside and out. I really enjoyed writing these chapters and truly hope you are able to benefit from them.

All too often I hear people moaning about life 'getting them down'; I challenge those people and anyone who feels the same to take the steps outlined in these chapters and to strip life to its simplest form. Looking after yourself: your mind, body and soul should be your top priority—only in this way can you truly strive for the highest realm of being your true self. If you achieve this, you will overcome the baseness of this earthly realm and travel great heights to reach the metaphysical and unseen realms. My sister, only then will you know the true potential of what has been gained and then will you reap the rewards not only in this life but for all eternity inshaAllah...

After all of this I discuss the rare gift of contentment and the final leg of our journey in an epilogue, to trust in Allah ﷻ because once you get to that point my dear, you'll realise nothing else actually matters.

Chapter Ten
The Importance of Self-Care

I believe self-care is not selfish for 'How can one serve from an empty vessel?'

When your husband walks into the house, gets changed (after an energy-boosting nap or some solitary time) and walks straight back out again to go to the gym (or to see a friend, run an errand, get a haircut... you get the picture!) and all you can think is, 'Well it's alright for you! You can just walk in and back out again!', my friends, it is time to realise that what you need is a good dollop of self-care.

I think it is important to realise the fundamental difference between looking after yourself because you need a bit of TLC and identifying the source of your problems if you're completely burnt out. If in fact it is the latter that is causing you undue stress, you need to look at what you're eating and drinking and also the balance of work, rest and play in your life. If there is a particular problem in your life that is usurping all of your energy, think about sharing this with a mentor or somebody you trust so that you can try to get to the bottom of it. Without dealing with the source of the issue, it will be difficult to change things with a bit of self-care.

If you're certain you don't have a problem at the source of your stress apart from needing to cut out a bit of time for yourself and you still need convincing that self-care is something that you need to invest in I advise you to conduct an experiment. Look after yourself, listen to your needs and attend to your self-care (this doesn't have to cost money at all! See below for examples) and then gauge your interaction with your loved ones. Have you got more time and patience for them? Are you more smiley? Do they get to see a good side of you? Someone who is less harassed, stressed or overwhelmed? Well, my dear, you've just had an experience of what self-care can do for yourself and your family!

You could put self-care in two categories. There is the self-care that makes you feel good immediately, and that which may take a bit of effort at the time but the rewards come afterwards, at the feeling of accomplishment of a job well done. Let's take the time to write a bit of a list so you have an idea what I'm talking about.

Self-care with Immediate Gratification:

- Have a bath/shower
- Take a nap
- Wash your hair
- Go for a walk
- Take time to listen to the birds singing/enjoy fresh air/ stop and smell the roses
- Phone a close family member or friend
- Meet up for a coffee/play-date
- Get dressed up and go out (or get taken out—even better!)
- Light a candle and pray/meditate, etc.
- Diffuse some essential oils, make yourself a bath using them or simply inhale from the bottle (I highly recommend doTerra oils for this!)
- Cooking/baking (if you enjoy this kind of thing)

- Reading
- Drawing/colouring/painting, etc.
- Exercise: yoga/pilates/swimming or an enjoyable low impact workout
- Go to a beautician for a facial/massage
- Go to a local spa for a manicure/pedicure/spa session

Self-care with Benefits Afterwards (in order to achieve a warm feeling of accomplishment):

- Cooking/baking (if you don't enjoy this kind of thing!)
- Exercise: a good tough workout to get that blood flowing
- Clean the house
- Laundry and ironing—catching up feels great!
- Clean out cupboards/drawers
- Rearrange things in the house/garden
- Necessary errands
- Visiting the elderly/sick (it's likely that you'll get a warm feeling during this activity too!)
- Helping out at a local hospice/hospital/care centre/school

I hope you can see here that the possibilities are endless according to the time you have, your interests and the resources you have in front of you.

I think what strikes one almost immediately about these lists (which are not exhaustive to say the least!) is the fact that you need time to carry these things out. Time is something of a limited resource in most households.

However, I do believe that time is the great equaliser. Everybody has twenty-four hours in a day. It's up to you how you use them.

Time management is very important and maybe taking the time to write out what you actually do *per hour of the day* may help you realise that there are parts of the day that you could use more mindfully to get more out of your limited time. Social media and binging on box sets come to mind here—ahem, yes I mean Netflix—and if you're using this as self-care, be mindful of each hour you spend on it and be aware of feeling even more drained and fatigued after watching because of the strain to your eyes, etc.

The other properties of self-care that I have not listed above are those things that you can do that don't take much time but can really change your perspective of the world. To remember to take it easy, enjoy the moment and take time to 'smell the roses' will be easier once you are being proactive with the physical self-care needs that are listed.

The ideas in this chapter are specifically for women who are left in charge of the children and household while the man works but it can just as easily be switched around for those of you with the opposite structure in the house. And I hope it goes without saying that these ideas can also be used for those singletons whom I know may have time but maybe also need a little nudge to spend it on themselves rather than others.

However, no matter what needs to be done in your day I'm asking you really nicely (OK, I'm TELLING you!) to use some of this time for yourself. It will make you more efficient. It will make you happier. It will make the time you spend with others sweeter and it will help you wave goodbye to your husband (if you found yourself agreeing with my first paragraph) when he leaves on that 'necessary errand' I mentioned earlier and to welcome him back with a loving smile when he returns. When you spend time on yourself, you tend not to begrudge people who do the same. You can be happy for them and then actually enjoy a sweeter relationship. *You are also free to give them and everybody else in your life the best of yourself.*

A few years ago, I spent four years exclusively homeschooling my daughter and my two subsequent sons. We went through various transitions with all three children at this time including two national house moves and two local ones (crazy, I know, and I wouldn't wish this upon anyone!) and *then* I was very blessed and honoured to be taken on a life-changing journey of the Hajj, alhamdulillah. Needless to say, I had a lot of time to reflect on that journey and when I came back, the most glaringly obvious solution (to the problem I didn't even know I had!) was *there was no need to be a martyr for the cause!* I immediately made the decision to stop homeschooling and to put my own needs first. I can't explain to you how liberating this was. This huge responsibility of the children's education and welfare for twenty-four hours of the day (and usually a six-day week on my own due to my husband's schedule at work) just disappeared and I felt a lot lighter for it.

Yes, there are many benefits of homeschooling but at that time it was too much for me to be a good wife, mother *and* teacher all at once. Something had to give. I decided that the children needed to go to school and I was better off for it. Since then I have carried out bouts of homeschooling whenever it has suited our situation and that's why I don't advocate either option. A school has many pros and cons, as does the decision to educate children at home. Each family just has to choose what best suits their child at the time—to nurture their interests and temperament is the best thing you can do for them. For more on this see Chapter Eight. For now, let's just say it's paramount to keep it flexible. Knowing that these decisions need not last forever does a lot to lessen the stress when deciding such things. Again, always try to be mindful of the choice you have.

Now, I will always try to remember to put myself first, otherwise I find that the people in my life will not necessarily get the *quality* of Sidra-time but just a huge *quantity* of it—and that isn't great for any of us.

Hopefully as you start to prioritise self-care in your life you'll find that your days will seem brighter, your energy levels higher, and you will not be as easily stressed out by daily life.

Maybe after reading this chapter, you realise that in order to move forward you have to put your own needs first. You will come to the realisation that this isn't selfish, but rather, it is essential for happy and healthy relationships. I think it's time to make self-care a priority.

Recently, I had chosen to involve myself in lots of rehearsals for a big sing-song and celebration, and because I have children of different ages, I wanted to give everyone a chance of taking part and decided to go to everything. Needless to say, I was completely burnt out after four or five weeks. I thoroughly enjoyed attending all the gatherings and get-togethers and appreciated the chance of being so heavily involved. However, through this experience I learnt a few things.

- Be aware that after all this excitement you need to give yourself time to recuperate, recharge and re-energise.
- Be aware that you'll be stretched to full capacity and therefore not your usual self.
- This kind of over-exertion can only be done on a short-term basis.

In light of the previous point, reassure close family members to let them know that you are aware you are taking on a lot and may be unduly stressed at times and not to take it personally!

Another important point is not to make huge life-altering decisions when feeling this way!

It's really interesting to note that the fact that this was a choice that I made for myself helped me to stay positive, motivated and get through, yet if somebody made me feel obliged to do the same thing I would expect a lot more sympathy and would, most likely, become bitter if I didn't get it. This is an example of how it wasn't the events that affected my mood, but the emotions that were attached to the events. Make self-care a part of your weekly routine so you can always be your best self.

It is so important to strive to have good character. About the Prophet ﷺ, Allah said:

'By the grace of Allah, you are gentle towards the people; if you had been stern and ill-tempered, they would have dispersed from round about you.'
[Quran 3:159]

This is a huge reminder of what good character can do to maintain important relationships. About himself, the Prophet ﷺ said:

'Allah has sent me as an apostle so that I may demonstrate perfection of character, refinement of manners and loftiness of deportment.'
[Muwatta]

By nature, he ﷺ was gentle and kind-hearted, always inclined to be gracious and to overlook the faults of others. Courtesy, compassion, tenderness, humility and sincerity were some of the keynotes of his character and we have a lot to learn from this. When fighting for justice, he could be severe but his severity was always balanced with generosity. He had charming manners which won him the affection of his companions.

A hadith states that 'when they met him they were in awe of him and when they knew him they fell in love with him.' How fortunate to have been one of them! As Talib al-Habib says in his beautiful nasheed describing the Prophetic beauty, what a wonderful way to be. May Allah, Most High, help us to emulate his beautiful character in the best way.

He never assumed an air of superiority, even when the Islamic Empire was growing and he had enough money (and every right) to behave in a superior manner. He didn't feel the need to show airs and graces as he had a true fear of Allah; humility was ingrained in his heart. Remember, self-care will also help you to take your character and disposition to the next level.

Be aware that you have choices (see the chapter on Choices for more information), and realise that it is healthy to maintain boundaries and make decisions so that you are not overstretched in any capacity through the decisions you have made in life. Always try to compensate for any loss of time to continue with self-care (whether it's beginning a job with long hours or deciding to home educate), by making time to look after yourself in order to reduce stress levels and recuperate from a hard day's work. This can be in the form of a nap straight after work, a daily schedule that includes 'quiet time' or 'non-contact' time if you're home educating, or a big mug of your favourite hot drink curled up with a book which you treat yourself to as soon as the kids are down for an early bedtime. Value your time and the time you give to others. Be mindful of giving others too much and not looking after yourself. It'll only make you bitter. Balance is key in this regard.

Be aware of what your Ultimate Self-Care Treat is. I think it is important to note here that if your work schedule has you feeling stressed, know yourself enough to identify a trigger that will help you to de-stress immediately. This may be an over-indulgent treat at your favourite coffee shop paired with blasting your best-loved qasidas in your car and/or going for a long drive with the kids. Whatever your ultimate self-care option is, use it to cope through those crazy, frazzled moments in your life when you need it the most. Remember, this isn't a regular treat or self-care option. It's your *ultimate*. Do it mindfully and without guilt. It is a rare pick-me-up that you know will work instantly to make yourself feel better. When times are difficult, use it to get through, sister.

Three Take-Home Points for Chapter Ten

1. Use some time for yourself. It will make you more efficient. It will make you happier.
2. Attaining good character traits is a huge part of being a good Muslim. Self-care is crucial to strengthen your character.
3. Make a list of your own self-care goals and look after yourself regularly. Your happiness will have a domino effect on your household and you will change lives and experiences.

Whatever you choose to do, make sure you look after yourself... because you're worth it!

Over the next few chapters, I will discuss how best to use the time you have in order to look after yourself in the best way.

Chapter Eleven
Tips for Time Management

In this chapter, I will list some fabulous ways which, if you adopt, will make you more efficient in using your time and more mindful of the time that you end up wasting.

The question that I get asked the most is how I get time to write a book and also run a big family household. Well, my thoughts are that everyone has time; it is the great equaliser, as I've mentioned before. Time is, in fact, all we've got! Everyone, no matter if you're royalty or a Bedouin traveller, has twenty-four hours a day and it is up to us what we do with them. Now, who doesn't need a few time-saving tips in this fast-paced age?

Thirty General 'Time Tips':

1. List tasks. This is the golden rule of time management. Each day, identify the two or three tasks that are the most crucial to complete in a day, and do these first.

Once you're done, the day has already been a success. You can move on to other things, or you can let them wait until tomorrow. You've finished the essentials.

2. Say 'No'. You need to learn to decline opportunities. Your objective should be to take on only those commitments that you know you have time for. This might mean you forsake something or an activity that is close to your heart for a time. Despair not; life is a cycle and everything is in phases. Sacrifice this for an easier week and you might find when things ease up a bit, you can bring it back and participate with energised vigour and love. (I've had to sacrifice time with my singing buddies recently and it was difficult to say the least. Boohoo!)

3. Sleep at least eight hours. Some people think sacrificing sleep is a good way to get more productivity out of the day. Sorry—this doesn't work and is actually counter-productive.

Most people need eight hours of sleep for their bodies and minds to function optimally. You know if you're getting enough—listen to your body, and don't underestimate the value of sleep.

It is recommended to get a good night's sleep and wake up early as opposed to sleeping late and rising late. See the chapter on Sleep for more on this. For now, I'd like to point out that a professor of neurology said: 'It could be psychological stress, eating at the wrong time for your body, not exercising enough, not sleeping enough, being awake at night by yourself or there maybe drug or alcohol use. There are a whole variety of unhealthy behaviours related to being up late in the dark by yourself.'

So, not only will it make you more time-efficient if you decide to become a 'morning lark', you can avoid lots of unhealthy side-effects of being up so late too! Hopefully the drug and alcohol use is not relevant to you or me but it is interesting to note nevertheless.

4. Form habits. Make a habit of the tasks you'd like to perform daily. Prayer would come into this, as would daily exercise routines. This makes each task become quite natural and enjoyable. Could you do something similar? Realise that 'a person is made up of his/her habits'. Try to employ long-term habits that will equal personal and spiritual growth and it'll optimise your day-to-day productivity.

5. Limit screen time. Time spent browsing social media, gaming or watching TV can be one of the biggest drains on productivity. I suggest becoming more aware of how much time you spend on these activities. By simply noticing how they're sucking up your time, you'll begin to do them less. Ironically, you can buy apps now that help you to do this! These help to monitor the time spent online so that you're more aware of it. You can also get apps that help you to mindfully decide not to touch your phone periodically throughout the day—this will help you to focus on the task at hand and to not get distracted. To discover the many benefits of digital free time, see Chapter Thirteen.

6. Leave some time between tasks. When we rush from task to task, it's difficult to appreciate what we're doing and to stay focused and motivated.

Allowing ourselves to relax for a short while between tasks can be a breath of fresh air for our brains. While taking a break, go for a short walk or perform some other mind-clearing exercise. Try to fit your tasks around prayer, rather than the other way round. This way your prayer will be less rushed, less of an afterthought and inshaAllah you will gain more from it.

7. Healthy lifestyle. Numerous studies have linked a healthy lifestyle with work productivity. Similar to getting enough sleep, exercising and eating healthily boost energy levels, clear your mind, and allow you to focus more easily. The Prophet Muhammad ﷺ said:

> 'There are two blessings, and most people evaluate these
> blessings incorrectly: Health and free time.'
> [Bukhari, Al-Riqaq]

8. One thing at a time. Only do the things that really matter. Slow down, notice what needs to be done, and concentrate on those things. Doing less things will create more value. Focus on quality rather than quantity. Our lives are full of too much of the things we don't need. When we can identify these and remove them, we become more and more in touch with what is significant and what deserves our time.

9. Maybe even lock yourself in. No distractions, no excuses. Sometimes, the only way you're going to get your work done is if you are under lock and key, alone in a room. However, given my responsibilities these days, this is more like a rare indulgence than a necessary procedure to finish my to-do list!

10. Speak to people who are very time-efficient. Notice how they prioritise certain tasks. Sometimes it is simply a change of mindset that will make you utilise each minute you have more effectively. Ask Allah ﷻ for barakah in your time.

11. Concentrate. Focus on the task at hand. Make every minute count. Close all other browser windows. Put your phone away, out of sight and on silent. Find a quiet place to work. Work on one task. Nothing else should exist. Immerse yourself in it.

12. Have fun. Efficiency is key and enjoyment can always be worked into your day. Work can be play. If you are already doing what you love, you can't go wrong!

13. Designate one area for the important stuff. Use one particular place to store keys, shoes, bags, coats, etc. This can be purpose-built or simply a convenient place that everybody is aware of. This way there is no last minute panic to find those essential items on the way out.

14. Satellite navigation. Use it when planning a new journey (also have a print-out or a book of maps) and make sure your phone is fully charged before you set off. Either that or double-check you have your phone charger in the car.

15. Beware of back-to-back appointments. If you have two appointments in one day, leave enough time to get to the second one with 15–20 minutes to spare. This will save you coming in late if an unknown incident then occurs to delay your journey.

16. Unexpected time on your hands. You have to be okay with 'dead' time that arises from showing up to an appointment early. This means that you have to learn how to fill the time when you arrive early for a meeting or show up to a doctor's appointment fifteen minutes ahead of time. Not only do you know how to use that time, you will use it productively. You can update a shopping list, respond to emails on your phone or you can clean out your handbag. If you're travelling with kids, get used to arriving early—have some simple healthy snacks at hand or a few books to look at to pass away the few minutes you might have to wait. This is better than planning to be exactly on time, as this means if something unpredictable and unavoidable happens (let's face it, it happens a lot with the little 'uns) you have enough leeway in order for it not to make you late. This means that you will arrive less frazzled if you are a little late and there is less stress in this situation.

17. Use your phone wisely. Use it to set alarms for real-life social appointments. Use it for reminders to call people back; cancel appointments; respond to emails or fill out essential forms for the children's school. Anything, really. I used it recently to remind myself to set off on time for one of my children's performances at school (and it really helped!). When you're having a busy day, just giving yourself a physical reminder to complete tasks in your quiet times means you'll end up being more organised.

18. Social media. Don't check it just before you're supposed to leave for somewhere. Be aware of seconds that turn to minutes that can make you late!

19. End tasks on time. Wrap things up if something is taking too long! This could be unplanned phone calls, visits, chats after the school run, etc. Make your apologies and explain you have things to do or people to see.

20. Become that organised person you've always aspired to be...

- Fill up your petrol tank
- Always have a snack with you
- Keep a pen within easy reach in your handbag
- Keep tissues and baby wipes in your car

Simply put, you will prevent the unknown last minute delays the best you can. If you are a mother of a young baby, you can fill up a baby bag and keep it next to the front door so that, even though you may have numerous children, you are ready to go at a moment's notice and you'll have all the essentials with you (including nappy rash cream and an extra pair of clothing including extra socks!).

21. Make plans. Plan dinner for the week and then use this info to plan your shopping. Plan a particular laundry day, vacuuming day (whole house) and shopping day—keep it the same every week. Be flexible if something comes up, (silently) plan in your head when you'll next get that job in and make sure you do it! This will help you to relax when you have some unscheduled free time and it will make you more efficient in the week.

22. Routines. Check *Flylady.net* for some fantastic tips on planning some fab daily, weekly and even monthly routines that will help you stay on top of everything in the house. Mindfully establish all routines. Make a checklist for the children to use until they get used to it and use drawings instead of writing for the younger ones.

23. Use a meal planner. You can get magnetic ones to put on your fridge these days too, yay! Here you can plan a weekly menu and can therefore do a very strategic shop based on what ingredients you need for each planned meal of the week. This will not only save money, but time and effort too, inshaAllah.

24. Use a calendar or noticeboard in a prominent area in the house. Make a habit of checking it every night for the following day to remind you about important dates and appointments. Talking about filling in forms for school, if you get a letter to sign, consider signing it *immediately* and hand it in straightaway. If this is not possible, sign it upon arrival at home and store it in the car or your coat pocket immediately so that you remember to hand it in the next day.

25. Use a personal diary/planner in the same way. Look for a pocket-sized one that you can fit in your handbag and remember to fill it in when you make those all-important appointments. Check it regularly. Tick tasks off as you complete them. Allow yourself to feel the buzz of the completion of a task.

26. Keep a small shoulder-bag packed with essential items. If you're like me and swap handbags every now and then (it definitely used to be all the time before my '*enoughism*' days!), try to keep essentials such as your phone, keys and purse together, which you can then stash into larger bags. This way as long as you keep your small bag packed with the right stuff, you know you have everything you need no matter which bag you're using.

27. Make the most of your natural daily quiet time. In the early mornings and late nights when children are still asleep, mums will find uninterrupted time more productive. When you have little ones, you can usually catch up on missed time by napping in the daytime with your children. If your children are a little older, you can retire to bed early, to catch up on that precious sleep.

28. Be aware of the time when you are the most productive and use that time effectively. You may be a morning lark or a night owl; you may find you're the most productive after an outdoor walk or a quick bout of exercise. Knowing when you are the most efficient will mean that you are able to be more productive in a shorter amount of time. All in all, we must learn to be more mindful of our time.

29. Stillness. In our forever technologically advancing world, a lot of people don't find time to just be still. Yet, it's extraordinary what a practice of stillness can do (see Chapter Fifteen). We are very blessed as Muslims to have five prescribed prayers in a day. Try to minimise distractions whilst praying by turning phones on silent and finding a quiet corner of the house to pray in. If this area of the house is always set up for prayer, all the better. Coming into that space will immediately calm you and act as a trigger to heighten your attention and focus on Allah, the Most High. Breathe deeply during the prayer as you change movements and slow everything down. Learn the meaning of the words you are uttering so that you can concentrate on what you're saying. Try to remember that you are in the presence of your Creator. Concentrate on making the most of the stillness of your mind, body and soul.

The Messenger of Allah ﷺ said when Angel Jibreel asked him about *ihsan*:

> '...You should serve Allah as though you see Him, for
> though you cannot see Him, He sees you.'

This way, when you go back to your daily tasks, you are fulfilled, rejuvenated and ready for the next job, with a renewed focus on the akhira and what's important inshaAllah.

Both action and its opposite, inaction, should play key roles in our lives. Discovering time in your life for silence reduces anxiety and shows you that there is no need to constantly rush. It also makes it easier to find your work pleasurable.

30. Keep looking for more tips and hacks. With the digital world rapidly evolving before our eyes it's important to keep learning. Keep your eyes peeled for more innovative ways to save time. And never underestimate the power of re-reading this list!

Three Take-Home Points for Chapter Eleven

1. Keep a balance. It's good to be productive and efficient but remember, giving yourself time to rest and recharge is crucial.
2. We are accountable for each moment here on Earth. Ask Allah ﷻ for help, specifically with using your time more effectively.
3. Be aware of the time when you are the most efficient and work smartly so that you are more productive in a shorter amount of time.

And now onto some tips for reducing that all-consuming stress in our lives.

Chapter Twelve
On Dancing and Other Ways to Reduce Stress!

*'Dance, when you're broken open. Dance, if you've torn
the bandage off. Dance in the middle of the fighting.
Dance in your blood. Dance when you're perfectly free.'*
[Rumi]

The dancing in this quote is that of the whirling dervishes, also known as the *sema*, which originated in the 13th century near Turkey. It is performed by *semazens* (whirlers) that belong to the Mevlevi sect of the Sufis. Sufism is the Islamic practice of attempting to achieve Divine knowledge and love though a personal relationship with God. Blood in the quote above is a metaphor for pain, be that spiritual or physical. The overall message is that you can dance through pain, which is a metaphor for the adversities one may face in life, when you're invoking the Divine at the same time. Through remembrance of Him your stress and pain will be alleviated inshaAllah. By performing the sema, Mevlevis try to experience the meaning of the words from the Quran:

*'To God belong the East and the West, and wherever you
turn is the face of God. He is the All-Embracing,
the All-Knowing.'*
[Quran 2:115]

Although I have used 'dancing' here as a metaphor to not take life seriously, we would do well to remember Allah ﷻ, through whatever means you wish (even dancing!), in times of hardship.

When it comes to movement and the remembrance of Allah ﷻ, it is a liberating sense of joy and freedom that one connects with Allah. There is sometimes a bit of confusion as to whether remembrance of Allah and dancing can go hand-in-hand. I hope to dispel your confusion with the following reports.

Anas (May Allah be pleased with him) reported that the Messenger of Allah ﷺ said:

> 'Once, the Abyssinians were dancing in front of the
> Messenger of Allah ﷺ, saying in their language:
> "Muhammad is a righteous servant." He ﷺ asked:
> "What are they saying?" It was said: "[They are saying]:
> "Muhammad is a righteous servant.""

Shaykh `Abdal-Qadir `Isa states:

> 'This hadith contains evidence that it is permissible to
> gather between permissible movement and exaltation
> of the Messenger of Allah ﷺ. It also proves that move-
> ment during remembrance is not described as forbidden
> dance, rather it is permissible because it energises the
> body for remembrance and assists one in having pres-
> ence of heart with Allah—if one's intention is sound.'
> [Ibid]

Shaykh Nuh Keller translates a lengthier passage from Imam Suyuti's *al-Hawi li al-Fatawi* in which he mentions the incident of Imam Ja`far:

'... and the hadith exists [in many sources, such as
Musnad al-Imam Ahmad, 1.108, with a sound (hasan)
chain of transmission] that Ja'far ibn Abi Talib danced
in front of the Prophet ﷺ when the Prophet told him,
"You resemble me in looks and in character," dancing
from the happiness he felt from being thus addressed,
and the Prophet did not condemn him for doing so, this
being a basis for the legal acceptability of the Sufis
dancing from the joys of the ecstasies they experience.'
[Keller, Sea without Shore]

So don't feel shy to dance even when you are happy, if you are moved by the ecstasies of joy received from your Creator!

When we are faced with a test or trial that we are finding truly difficult, remember that the point of life is to return to our Creator in the best state possible, through living a life of faith with a sound heart and good works. Experiencing some type of loss or difficulty is often the way Allah, the Most High, brings our attention back to Him and our purpose.

These illnesses or losses are sometimes simply a test. They don't always imply that someone is bad, or cursed or being punished. When these tests come we need to understand their purpose, and realign our hearts to the Divine and not stray from our ultimate goal. Allah, the Most High, says:

'Do you expect to enter Paradise without being tested,
like those before you [were]?'
[Quran 2:214]

'And We will most certainly test you until we know
which amongst you are those who strive and those who

are patient, and so We can bring out your true qualities.'
[Quran 47:31]

This time on earth and these trials and tribulations will soon be a thing of the past. Those who accept this sooner often do better through the difficulties they face; they are not reduced to being afraid, face depression or give in to despair due to the inevitable trials of life.

So, we need to remember to have a long-term perspective about whatever trials and tribulations we face in life. Even in our worldly life, failure often guides us towards the successful path which we end up taking. The concept of failure teaches us to learn and grow and helps us to ultimately succeed (as long as we don't give up in the meantime!). Never see failure as a barrier that cannot be surpassed; rather, see it as a sign to take a detour. Maybe you won't get to your destination by the quickest route that you have planned, but rather you'll get to it via the route that Allah ﷻ has planned. The one which only He knows is best for your life, your soul and ultimately your growth and knowledge of Him. Initially we'll be disheartened because it's not what we have planned. Rather, it is what Allah has planned and how can His Plan falter when it has been written by the Best of Writers?

When things are getting you down, maybe you could begin a lighthearted hobby, kick around the football with the kids or sit down to read a humorous book. Life is full of great moments; try your best to enjoy them. Remember your Ultimate Self-Care Treat? Use it for moments of intense stress. Don't use it because you've lost control. Use it mindfully to gain control!

Reading *Ayat al-Kursi* also helps in times of stress. The translation is nothing less than empowering:

'Allah! There is no god but He, the Living, The Self-sub-sisting, Eternal. No slumber can seize Him nor sleep. His are all things in the heavens and on earth. Who is there that can intercede in His presence except as He permitteth? He knoweth what (appeareth to His crea-tures as) before or after or behind them. Nor shall they compass aught of his knowledge except as He willeth. His throne doth extend over the heavens and on earth, and He feeleth no fatigue in guarding and preserving them, For He is the Most High. The Supreme (in glory).'

No doubt, there is a balance created in the heart when you remind yourself who is in charge. Don't take life so seriously. I know it's one of those pieces of advice that's easy to spout and hard to execute, but honestly, it's a life-changer. Try to stay lighthearted when things go a bit pear-shaped.

Remember when you were younger and you'd get ice cream in your hair and you'd laugh it off? Remember stepping into a puddle up to your knee and feeling gleeful rather than awful?

Your perception of an event can change according to your perspective. Let's attach the emotions of silliness, joy and aban-donment when the kids do something a little naughty. Maybe you and your husband can exchange a quick, surreptitious amused glance before you 'act' angry and tell the child off for their misbehaviour. Playfulness and a lighthearted attitude can carry you over a heavy cloud of stress as easily as a hot air bal-loon rises over a green field.

If your toddler gets a bowlful of yoghurt all over his fresh-ly washed jumper and you forget to smile, remind yourself of that girly nature that guided you to chase ducks in the park and wade through the mud to get to the lake! If you were never that inclined to get dirty yourself, think about the fact that this little thing won't matter in a few minutes when everyone is tidied up. The dirt or food can be washed off but the memories will last a lifetime.

Everything becomes lighthearted and more fun when you embrace the moment and enjoy the silly (or annoying!) antics of the children or the husband before they are gone (hopefully just the children!) and all you have left are memories. Why taint the short time that you have together?

Having said all this, I do understand it's difficult to maintain a lighthearted demeanour when the child (or husband!) is purposely messing around, when the teenager is rude or dinner is delayed and it seems to be one of those days. In this case, you'll want to tell them off but try to keep anger at bay and calmly remind them to do what's right. Try to use positive language, for example, telling them what you want them to do rather than telling them what not to do. You'll be thankful for this later. Also it's a good time to practise anger management. There are two important points to remember in this endeavour.

- Take some time out and make wudu. The Holy Messenger ﷺ has said:

> 'Anger comes from the devil, the devil was created of
> fire, and fire is extinguished only by water; so when one
> of you becomes angry, he should perform ablution.'
> [Abu Dawud]

- Take a few deep breaths and take steps to physically calm yourself down. The Messenger of Allah ﷺ said: 'If any of you becomes angry and he is standing, let him sit down, so his anger will go away; if it does not go away, let him lie down.'

If you can't remind yourself to remain happy in moments of madness you're not showing much affection to yourself and those around you.

This is a reminder to remember to laugh at yourself when you get things wrong. Make your intention to be lighthearted in life; an intention to 'dance' and make it through, no matter what happens.

Now what is really interesting here is that your ability to be lighthearted is affected by your stress levels. Have you ever been in the position where little things are getting to you? Or do you know somebody who's usually so laid-back and relaxed but lately they seem to be getting annoyed at every little thing? This is an indicator of high stress levels. Maybe you're the kind of person who can't relax during the week when you're really busy, or maybe you can't manage to relax even when you're on holiday—this will affect your ability to laugh and 'dance' through when things do not go as expected.

I have recently gone down a dress size (and I am trying really hard to maintain it, but more about that later), and have been reading up on the Louise Parker method which I think is fantastic. The best part of the book for me was the realisation that weight loss goes hand-in-hand with living a better life and therefore is synonymous with 'living your best life in your best body'. In Louise Parker's book *Lean For Life: Transform your body in 6 weeks, Protect the results forever*, she speaks about two other aspects that need to change as well as endorsing a mindful diet and an intelligent workout routine. These are:

- Think successfully
- Live well

As part of the 'Live Well' section, she speaks about sleeping properly, reducing screen time (especially before bedtime) and reducing stress levels, and how that's so important to leading a healthy life and how it also significantly improves the chance of losing weight. 'Dancing' through life is much easier to do when you aren't being dragged down with the stress of it all.

There are low levels of stress and there are high levels. Low levels are just so irritating. Some people may call these First World Problems. It's when your cleaner breaks a favourite vase, a child spills milk all over the floor just as you were about to leave for the school run, when your son rubs Sudacrem all over the bedroom carpet or you lose your car keys for the umpteenth time. Your heartbeat is at a high rate and you find you have a terribly short temper. Here is the interesting part:

Some days can be filled with small stresses and nothing will ruin your mood, and on others just one little thing can be really difficult to handle. This only happens if you're already dealing with high levels of chronic stress due to an unrelated cause.

So the ability to handle and deal with chronic stress significantly reduces the *effect* of these small stresses. When you feel that you have chronic stress, do your utmost to correct the situation. You can't ignore it! There is no way things will get better if you let things go without dealing with them.

It is a misconception that stress increases weight loss. This is only true for those rare, shocking events in life—the illnesses, the life-changing property loss, etc. In actual fact it is the constant high and low level stresses together that cause *weight gain*.

How to reduce stress:

- You are what you eat. Eat well. Think low carbs rather than low fat and eat your greens.

- Stay active. I have found success using the Fitness Blender workout videos. (See *FitnessBlender.com* to try one yourself).
- Practise self-care.
- Meditate/pray/schedule some quiet time for at least 20 minutes every day
- Declutter. Look at the things you've accumulated and try to be ruthless about what you need to keep and what you can live without. A clutter-free life helps attain clarity of mind. An item you own can be either useful or beautiful. Make a decision, fill up those bags and put them straight into your car boot so that you can give them to your local charity shop as soon as you get a chance. Remember it's not wasting if another person is able to reuse or recycle it, and if it aids lifting your brain fog to make you more productive then it's definitely worth it!
- Let it go. If something is stressing you out, make a decision and then leave it to Allah. To constantly think about it and worry about whether things work out is detrimental to your health and stress levels. You've done what you can, let go of all doubts, trust in Allah ﷻ that He'll do what's best. There are two things you can do. The first is to read or listen to the Quran. There have been studies done to prove that listening to a melodious recitation of the Holy Quran evens out your breathing and helps to reduce stress. You can also use the old adage of sending peace and a prayer to our beloved Prophet Muhammad ﷺ every time a stressful thought comes back into your head. Works every time.
- Talk positively about changes you will make.
- Write down what you want to get out of each day. This can change according to the season, children's school routine vs holiday time, etc.

- Remember my chapter on friends? Choose good company. You need to be aware of the effect people in your life have on you. Recognise those who celebrate who you are, those who encourage you and bring motivation and fun into your life. Think about who you spend most of your time with. If you're spending time with competitive, negative people who don't back your dreams, you risk not realising your own dreams and goals. It isn't a conducive environment to reach your potential and is definitely not a good environment to be in to reduce your stress levels either.

- Create a support group. Find a group of people who want to achieve the same goals as you, be it a writing group, a slimming group or even a devotional or religious group. Being around people who have the same goals as you will significantly improve your own chance of achieving success.

- If you are shy of a big support group, pick one person instead. Having one accountability partner will significantly improve your chances of straightening out that aspect of your life which you focus on. This person will help to keep you on track by checking up on you to see if you've reached your daily or weekly targets.

- I hope and pray these tips on reducing stress will help you 'dance' through life and help you to remember how to draw from your more 'lighthearted self' when things don't go the way you've planned.

- Reducing and managing stress is a huge part of life. Indeed, it is a trick that will keep you sane through times of emotional distress and hardship. Don't forget to 'Live in day-tight compartments' as Dave Carnegie said in his book *How to Stop Worrying and Start Living*. Remember, this was what helped me through the physical and emotional trauma of breaking my wrist a few months after I had my fifth baby.

To live each day 'in the moment', whilst trying not to worry about what the past means or what the future holds is what it entails. Your intention is to get through the day. It minimises stress and worry through narrowing your perspective and allowing you to get on with the practical aspects of the day. Sure, at one point you'll need to sit down and work out a solution to the situation at hand. You'll find that (and Dave mentions this in his book too) once you've stopped worrying the solution will come more easily.

There is a prayer that is recommended in times of dire stress and need. It is called *Salat al-Hajja* or The Prayer of Need. It is read at a time of dire need and its wording is very beautiful and calming in itself. Abdullah ibn Abi Awfa (May Allah be pleased with him) relates that the Messenger of Allah ﷺ said:

> '*Whoever has a need with Allah, or with any human being, then let them perform ritual ablutions well and then pray two rakats. After that, let them praise Allah and send blessings on the Prophet ﷺ. After this, let them say: There is no God but Allah the Clement and Wise. There is no God but Allah the High and Mighty. Glory be to Allah, Lord of the Tremendous Throne. All praise is to Allah, Lord of the worlds. I ask you (O Allah) everything that leads to your mercy, and your tremendous forgiveness, enrichment in all good, and freedom from all sin. Do not leave a sin of mine (O Allah), except that you forgive it, nor any concern except that you create for it an opening, nor any need in which there is your good pleasure except that you fulfill it, O Most Merciful!*'

And no matter what you're going through, don't forget:

'Surely, Allah is with the Patient.'
[Quran 2:153]

Three Take-Home Points for Chapter Twelve

1. Remember Allah ﷻ, through whatever means you wish (even dancing!) in times of hardship. It will help alleviate your pain.
2. Eat well, stay active, practise self-care, meditate. This will all help to reduce stress in your life.
3. The concept of failure teaches us to learn and grow and helps us to ultimately succeed (as long as we don't give up in the meantime!). Never see failure as a barrier that cannot be surpassed; rather, see it as a sign to take a detour.

Now, for a discussion on reducing the negative impact that digital technology can have on your life.

Chapter Thirteen
Limiting Wi-Fi and Social Media

I know you don't want to hear this. Trust me, it's difficult to write too, because I know what this addiction feels like.

> *'Interactive wireless mobile devices, computer games*
> *and social media can exert a powerful influence on the*
> *brain like other addictive substances such as tobacco,*
> *sugar and heroin.'*
> ['Psychological Issues and Digital Technology Use',
> a paper written by Dunckley, Eberle, Golomb etc.]

Use of the internet has many detrimental effects, many of which are cited in this paper, from psychological and physiological effects on the central nervous system to the negative impact on a child's development and behaviour. Even a parent's ability to parent effectively becomes questionable.

Listen up to what we can do about this because, by now, something from the world wide web surely has you in its clutches. You may have resisted WhatsApp for a while but now the school parent group is on there and there is stuff you're missing; you relent. Maybe Facebook didn't do it for you and you didn't really see what the fuss was about but now you're constantly checking Twitter, find yourself giggling at the GIFs people send and are constantly shocked at the news and celebrity gossip of the world. Maybe not. Maybe you have certain 'important' WhatsApp groups you have a loyalty to and can't give up. Or maybe you feel there is no harm in screen time and you applaud yourself on the quiet time it gives you in a household full of children. Who said parenting is hard?

Well, it's time to admit, the internet is a time usurper and a physiological game-changer and sooner or later you will have to face up to the effects it is having on you and your family. Not only can your use of it affect your immediate family, your friends, your relatives, but it can negatively impact relationships at large and an addiction to this is something to be wary of indeed. Your children may need your attention but because of your constant use of the phone, you are unaware of the reality that you give more attention to this device than your nearest and dearest. In fact, your relationship with those closest to you is likely to have an irreversible detrimental effect if you don't wake up and take things into hand right now.

To stop this snowballing effect, let me give you a head's up on the detriment it is causing in our brains.

You'll find that the more time you spend on it, the more your body forms happy chemicals in your brain, the more your brain craves these chemicals, the more time you spend on it and so it becomes a vicious cycle.

Social media provides a constant barrage of rewards (such as the brain's happy chemical dopamine) for very little effort so the brain begins to rewire itself—making you desire these rewards. You rarely get a break and therefore are unable to get back to your 'baseline' of dopamine. You begin to crave more and more of this neurological excitement after each interaction for a deeper 'hit'. Much like the behaviour of the brain after taking drugs. Scary. To put an end to this, try a digital detox.

A Digital Detox

This includes switching off all mobiles, smartphones, tablets, laptops and computers for a certain length of time. This enables you to spend screen-free time doing whatever you enjoy. A digital detox is also a chance to recharge and rest. A digital detox should ideally be around twenty-four hours as a minimum.

The last time I decided to do a digital detox was in Ramadan. A spiritual detoxification if you will, of life as we know it in this world.

As everyone knows, the last ten days are the most blessed days and nights of Ramadan and everyone does their utmost to make the most of these fleeting days before Ramadan is over, once again. It has been reported that:

> *'Once the last ten [days of Ramadan] started, the*
> *Messenger of God ﷺ used to spend the nights in*
> *worship, wake his family, strive, and tighten his belt.'*
> [Bukhari, Muslim]

'Tighten his belt' refers to the Messenger of Allah ﷺ increasing his determination. With this in mind, many people take to leaving their worldly cares and matters and retreat into a room or a mosque for the entirety of the ten days. Usually, they have minimal contact with people and concentrate on reading the Quran and learning about Islam through reading or listening to talks, etc.

I had the idea of spending the last few days of this precious month mobile-phone-less. I remember that when I asked my second eldest son if he thought I could do it, he replied, 'That's easy! I do that every day, Mum!' Haha. Then, I asked my eldest son what he thought. 'I challenge you to do it, Mum!' he said, with a cheeky glint in his eye. Hmm.

I also decided to give up wi-fi completely. After feeling very apprehensive—I mean, what if someone needed to contact me in an emergency? And what about important stuff I could listen to via the good old World Wide Web? I decided I should just do it. I reminded myself that there are other ways of getting in touch (such as landlines, remember those?) and that I could learn stuff the old-fashioned way, through books and CDs. I reflected that the hardest thing would be not being in contact with my lovely international sisters and their families... but it wasn't for long and I hoped to be a better person once I came out the other side. So, concentrating on the fact that it should be a good outcome and totally worth it, I marched on.

It wasn't like I was on my phone all the time, but I was aware that it would free up time if I didn't feel the need to check my messages and email account throughout the day! I thought that limited wi-fi usage would hopefully help me to be more creative with my time. It would be nice to actually read one or two of the couple of hundred books we have on our shelves! Also, I remembered what it was like going on trips to remote places in Wales or Scotland and there was no network. It was so liberating. With this intention, I hoped to reproduce that feeling.

I went ahead and did it. Here are some reflections *after* my digital detox:

Prior to this detox, when I first downloaded WhatsApp Messenger, I had wanted to keep in touch with my international and national family members. I remember what a buzz it was to have an instant group conversation with family members across the world. However, after my detox, I've found that it's a huge time usurper!

Being a mother (read: Manager of the Household), I've often thought how little time I have for myself. I try to cut out a weekly slot for my writing, which I sometimes can't keep, and people are still surprised that I make time for it. Yes, it is surprising. In this digital world, a moment of stillness is a rare moment. Yet, we will learn in Chapter Fifteen the numerous benefits of stillness, not to mention that the learned Sufi master and poet says:

> 'Stillness is the language of God.
> Everything else is poor translation.'
> [Rumi]

When cutting out certain things from my life including WhatsApp, I became aware of the fact that being in touch with everyone all of the time didn't necessarily work for me.

Let me explain. There's a point in an Enid Blyton book where Quentin, George's father, fed up of the phone ringing all day exclaims (something like) 'We're at the mercy of this phone!' Nowadays, I feel we all are! I was driving the other day and missed a call. When I stopped the car, I managed to call back straight away. I was then asked why I didn't pick up the phone.

'I was driving,' I said.

'Well, have you not got Bluetooth? That way you could pick up your calls!'

'I don't want to pick up my calls whilst I'm driving! I can just about manage the kids and drive at the same time, God knows what would happen if I throw a phone call in there too!' There was agreement and laughter. But it really made me think.

Is it just me or do you also feel it's totally unreasonable that someone should either answer a call, reply to a message instantly or have to justify why they haven't done so every single time somebody gets in touch with them? It's madness!

Unless you tell everyone you're offline for a few days. *Then* it's total freedom, a blissfully liberating feeling. Well, that's once you've got the withdrawal symptoms out of the way! This took about seven days for me. Yes, seven days of my fingers itching to check my messages whenever I handled my phone— that's whenever I checked the time, messaged (using normal messenger) or used the satellite navigation on journeys, etc. I allowed myself to use SeekersHub and YouTube for Quran. I also checked my email every few days, after I realised I might miss school messages. But apart from that I was offline and I was very surprised that it took me that long to be completely comfortable with it.

It made me feel like I wasn't able to make an independent decision about my own health and betterment without being completely firm in it. I had less control than I thought I had over the matter because, without me fully realising it or inviting it in, it had become a massive part of my life (whether I liked it or not) and to pull away would take more strength, commitment and dedication than I had ever imagined I would need.

To help me in resisting the temptation to use my phone again I would reward myself in a small way every day. Time with a favourite book, a few indulgent biscuits with tea or even per- mission to buy myself a small gift kept me going! Happy times. I knew how monumental this decision was and that if I was to control my desires on this front I would feel a magnitude of ben- efits.

After this initial struggle, I cannot explain to you how light I felt. I found five things:

1. **Mindfulness.** I became more mindful of the time I had in between doing my jobs for the day.
2. **More time.** I found I had pockets of time to actually get things done that I hadn't been able to squeeze in before. I don't know about you, but I assumed a few minutes here and there didn't take up much time, but such is this digital

device that once it's in your hands, it has a way of getting you to click, click, click, and before you know it, time has passed!

3. **I needed to go back to my phone serving me.** There is a lot of ease if used sparingly; checking messages when I'm in a rush or trying to do something else really doesn't help!

4. **Excellent for my nafs (ego).** My thoughts/comments are not as important as I thought! Sometimes, I read something and then feel I need to add something to the discussion. My reply will sometimes be written to every message that I have a thought about! (I realise everyone isn't like this. Lucky you!). Not only is this time consuming, during my detox I came to the conclusion that the WhatsApp world will go round without my thoughts/comments/opinions about every point in discussion.

5. **I generally felt happier.** I was able to live in the moment. Not automatically checking my messages every time I checked the time freed me to be more present in the moment and enjoy the here and now. It meant that I was readjusting my baseline of dopamine to a new level so I was able to enjoy the little things in life again. My brain rewired itself, if I may say so, and it was easier to get a hit of dopamine from witnessing everyday things.

As a conclusion, I would say that I am now more mindful of the time I use on the internet. I am trying to limit WhatsApp to twice a day. I have recently installed an app on my phone called '*Moment. Less Phone. More Real Life.*' which really helps me become mindful of the time I'm using on the net and helps me remember to reduce it when I can. There are probably lots more like this; have a look and see what you find. Remember, there's no need to give it up completely. Being aware of the effects and reducing the time spent on the net is a fabulous start. Take small steps and soon you'll find yourself back in control with the internet serving you as and when you need it. After all, that's what we all want, isn't it? Don't forget to reward yourself for every baby step you manage to achieve. Enjoy taking back control of your life and your time!

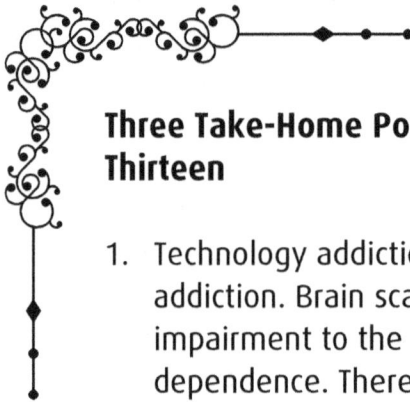

Three Take-Home Points for Chapter Thirteen

1. Technology addiction is a psychological addiction. Brain scans show a similar impairment to the brain to those with drug dependence. There is a degradation of white matter in the brain, which hinders emotional processing, decision making and attention.
2. Make time for yourself with a 'Digital Detox'. Switch off all mobiles, smartphones, tablets, laptops and computers for a certain length of time. This enables you to spend screen-free time doing whatever you enjoy.
3. Experiencing a digital detox will free you to be more present in the moment and enjoy the here and now, which will lead to increased gratitude in the long run.

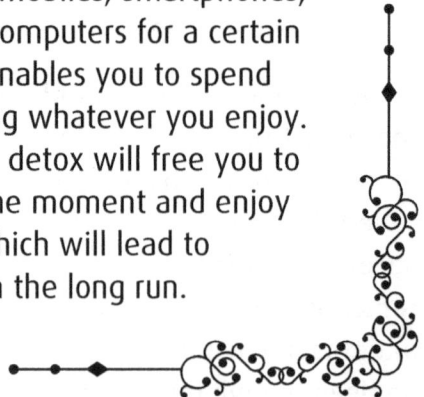

Next, we will look at healthy eating and exercise. These are two arenas that, if sorted, help to facilitate everything else in your life in a beautiful way. Read on to find out more.

Chapter Fourteen
Healthy Eating and Exercise

So, where shall we start? There is so much to say on the topic of healthy eating that I thought it would be a good idea to read and reflect on a few reminders of the tradition of the Prophet ﷺ. Among this guidance is that:

- Your body is a trust, and it has rights over you.
- One should learn the specific sunnahs of eating—such as beginning in the name of Allah, eating with one's right hand, praising good food but not criticising any food, to finish eating before one's fill, praising Allah after eating, and to learn what specific foods the Prophet ﷺ particularly praised with an intention to increase one's love for him.
- One must eat enough so that their physical and mental strength will not be diminished.
- One should not overeat. Eating more than required is disliked, and prohibited when harmful. Celebrations which are few and far between are recognised as times of joy and thankfulness and are not seen harmful.
- Eat well and within limits and thank God for His blessings.
- Eat with others, and invite others to share one's food. There is a great reward in hosting others. We know that

in Ramadan the reward is greater and, in any case, to feed guests is an honour and comes with many hidden blessings.

- Eat slowly, chew one's food well and wait to swallow before taking another bite. This is also excellent for digestion; indeed, latest scientific research has shown that the slower one eats the more enzymes are released in the stomach to aid digestion. Also, it takes the stomach around twenty minutes to tell the brain that it's full, so if you're eating more slowly you're less likely to overfill your stomach.

Remembering such sunnahs will increase the blessings when eating and will be better for your health inshaAllah.

Body image is a huge factor in determining your perceptions of your own body's attractiveness, health, acceptability, and functionality from early childhood. This body image continues to change and grow as you age and receive feedback from peers, family members, colleagues at work, etc.

It is so important to stay away from perfectionism and self-criticism as this can influence the development of a negative image of your body. Look out for signs such as:

- Obsessive self-scrutiny in mirrors.
- Thinking disparaging comments about your body and frequently comparing yourself with other people.
- Envy of a friend's body or the body of a celebrity (any type of envy is unhealthy, the best thing is to make dua for that person).

Factors such as lifestyle, diet and exercise all play a role in determining how one looks. It is so important to remain fit and healthy; your perception of your own body will become more positive as you learn to look after yourself and become happier in your own skin. More often than not, if you're taking care of your inside, your outside will glow with health and you will naturally look your best. Exercising regularly helps flush toxins from the body and makes one look and feel better.

Let's go on to discuss my experiences regarding dieting and exercise. As I've mentioned previously, alhamdulillah, I have recently dropped a dress size and have been working hard to keep it off. However, I had not been looking forward to writing this chapter, as my life began to become increasingly busy and my priority to keep this excess weight off was slowly decreasing. My baby was growing up to become a walking, babbling toddler which meant that I was constantly running around after him, entertaining him, cleaning up after him and generally not getting much of a chance to sit down and reflect on looking after myself and my own needs. Eating food on the go and snacking, without much preparation, became a habit. My older children helped a lot with my youngest child and I'm very grateful for that, but when we were on our own however, on a normal school day, I found it hard to make time for myself. Any diet that required regular exercise or specially prepared meals went out the window. However, I am happy to report that things then took a turn for the better. I began afresh and with new vigour and determination decided to make healthy choices and to look after my body again.

Let me first explain that, like with many other things, the first step is recognising that there is a problem and making the intention to do something about it. Once you have got to this point, congratulate yourself—it's a good place to be! Fifty percent of success is marked by the admission that there is a problem in the first place. There are many factors to consider, not only what food goes into your body but where the ingredients have been sourced from and the amount of water you drink to the balance of nutrition you have on your plate.

I've recently been intermittently fasting, or 'fake fasting' as my children call it, because I'm allowed to drink for sixteen hours out of twenty-four. The fabulous thing is that you can count your hours asleep as part of this fast too! If you want to find out more about this method, check out the 'Keto diet'. This method is actually not outlined in the books recommended at the end of this book (but there are plenty of websites on this). It is another strategy I have adapted to help me to eat healthily and strive to look after my body. An outline follows:

Within this there is an option to 'fake fast', where one is allowed to drink water or any hot drink but should steer away from milk (because of the lactose it contains). A 'bulletproof' coffee is recommended first thing in the morning. This consists of instant coffee, double cream, butter, coconut oil and hot water from the kettle. The idea is to fill yourself up with a 'fatty' drink but one that doesn't require your body to produce insulin, as it doesn't contain sugar or carbohydrates. In fact, the basis of this diet or way of eating, is to give your body a break from producing insulin for sixteen hours a day. Of course, the Prophet ﷺ fasted and encouraged all Muslims to fast regularly, the benefits of which are many. If you are able to fast (and not just fake it) then I'd encourage you to do that regularly as a part of a healthy eating programme.

In this method, your body kicks into ketosis when you're fasting. Ketosis is the metabolic process of using fat as the primary source of energy instead of carbohydrates. This means your body is directly breaking down its fat stores as energy instead of slowly converting fat and muscle cells into glucose for energy. You enter ketosis when your body doesn't have enough glucose (sugar or carbohydrates) available. The prime function of the ketogenic diet is to put the body in ketosis.

Ketones are byproducts of the body breaking down fat for energy that occurs when carbohydrate intake is low. Using ketosis has many benefits like:

- Weight loss
- Improved energy levels
- Increased mental focus
- Longevity and disease prevention
- Increased physical performance

Research has also shown that by following this diet, people with Type 2 diabetes have been known to reverse their diagnosis.

Knowledge of these healthy eating programmes is actually really beneficial—even if one doesn't seem moved to do anything at all (at first). Like I said, the first step is acknowledging there's a problem. Maybe sometimes, culturally, we give ourselves excuses for the extra weight we put on. For example: We're getting older and our metabolism slows down, we're naturally less active as we feel less energetic or we assume that because some of us are mothers, we are meant to be heavier.

In South Asian culture, to be 'heavy' translates to being healthy and strong and the elders look down at mothers who are slight or very slim. They perceive them as weak, without the strength it takes to raise children. Let's try to get away from this mindset. We can be lean and strong. Strength comes from training our muscles and not by getting bigger and eating too much!

We have to admit that contrary to popular belief, we do have control over these matters. If one follows a set diet and exercise programme, one is likely to reverse the symptoms of ageing. The Jason Vale book on juicing has a testimonial in it that states that a couple found their grey hair turning back to their natural colour, through juicing every day! Through good nutrition and regular movement, people are able to maintain a great standard of brain health and agility, no matter what their age.

A Word on Stretchy Waistbands

With the increasing girth of people in the UK, is it me, or are stretchy waistbands more common in the shops than ever? Be aware that you are in danger of letting things go by wearing these all the time! This is because you'll be unaware of your true weight or size and it will be difficult to nip a problem in the bud. Weight creeps up slowly and it's easier to keep a handle on it when trousers cease to zip up, or when the next notch on the belt is now in use!

I remember when I was younger and I watched some of my friends dieting. Being naturally slim and unable to eat when I wasn't hungry, I didn't have to grapple with diets and weight issues at that time. I actually remember being so grateful, thinking that the determination and single-mindedness it takes to lose weight is something I couldn't ever imagine possessing, so I was glad I didn't have to.

Then I had children.

I had to do something and honestly, it wasn't too difficult the first or second time I had to lose my baby weight, but as the years went by and my body kept morphing after becoming pregnant and then giving birth, it became harder and harder to get rid of the extra fat. Through breastfeeding, rather than losing weight like some women do, I actually found I was even hungrier than usual and over-compensated by more than likely eating over the five hundred daily calories one is known to lose! Then after a close family death, I found that I was simply piling it on and stretch pants became my friends and I didn't have a strong enough mindset to lose it once again. Honestly, I truly realised what it felt like to just give in.

And that's when I became pregnant for the last time. I did allow myself to give in to the sweet cravings a little, but then I also had a good reason to start watching what I ate again, as a small fetus was growing inside me and I tried to be mindful of what was passing through the umbilical cord. Thankfully, with another pregnancy and labour looming, I also had a huge reason to remain active and found that this was enough to curb my appetite and put a stop to my weight gain; the Louise Parker Method was so inspiring for me at this point in life. Not only did I feel that her philosophy of remaining active and being mindful made a huge difference, I also found that I enjoyed reading about maintaining a holistic healthy approach to life (I especially enjoyed buying new crockery to encourage myself to eat beautiful foods in it! Hehe). Like everything else, healthy eating and exercise go well with a healthy mind and therefore a stress-free and happy life. It's all connected.

My husband found success losing weight and maintained it after reading *Wheat Belly* (see Recommended Reading at the end of the book) and I've got to admit that when I read about the fact that the food industry is made to increase our appetites and make us consume more food, I was so happy that the blame was shifting from my own lack of self-discipline to the ingredients purposely put into our foods to make us crave more sugar and carbs. I noticed that once I lowered my carb intake, my appetite for carbs actually decreased! I was able to go for longer periods without eating at all. It felt like nothing less than a miracle. Processed foods are full of these craving-enticing ingredients. This includes branded bread. Bread made in a bakery is always better and contains fewer ingredients. This is why I put *Not On the Label* on the reading list. If you stick to making food from scratch, like our ancestors did, then you will surely benefit from cutting out the extra chemicals and ingredients your body doesn't need.

Think of trying to get more greens and good fats into your diet; all this advice about swapping butter for margarine to lower cholesterol is now redundant. The natural stuff is what's best—stick to that.

A great blender is a fantastic investment. Green smoothies are a great way to get your daily fruit and veg portion down you. I don't always stick to the apportioned 'five-a-day' but I've found that smoothies can easily replace an unhealthy snack and, actually, by adding a green smoothie to your diet you naturally attract the good stuff. Seriously, try it for yourself. If you find it difficult to break out of sweet and carbohydrate comfort food cravings, then simply *add* a green juice or smoothie to your diet and see what happens. I would say the same about kefir. Simply *adding* a cup of kefir to your diet not only helps maintain a healthy gut flora, but also lessens the cravings. Kefir is a probiotic yoghurt drink, full of friendly bacteria that eases digestive issues and is also very refreshing. You can make it at home, if you can get hold of some kefir grains (these are usually pretty easy to get hold of from anyone who makes it at home themselves as the grains multiply during production), otherwise you can buy a ready-made kefir yoghurt drink from your local Polish shop or even your local supermarket.

Food and exercise go hand-in-hand. The most benefit I've found in maintaining a healthy lifestyle is when I've paired healthy eating with regular exercise. Not only does it encourage one to eat even more healthily, the results are manifest in the mind and soul too, subhanAllah. And then you also get the added benefits of healthy skin, hair, nails and bones! You can't go wrong.

Let's Talk About Exercise!

Exercising is essential to maintaining a healthy body and mind. Meeting a buddy in the park, a weekly exercise class or a bout at the gym is a wonderful way to remain active in order to look after your body. If you find time is short or, like me, it's difficult to get out to attend a gym because of childcare then use an online exercise class. I've used 'Fitnessblender.com' very successfully and recommend it to all. You can mix and match routines and warm ups, you can adjust the timings and routines to suit yourself and you can do all this from the comfort of your home. Make yourself a routine of exercise and you'll get rid of that mind-fog and it really helps motivate you to eat well too. Team up with a support group to help keep you on the right track. Having some accountability will make a huge difference in attaining that goal.

And then, why spoil all that good work and eat sweet treats afterwards?! Your workout will actually help you build up and maintain your willpower. You'll find that the more you exercise, the more likely you are to show greater willpower in other areas of your life. Studies have been done to show that the greater the amount of exercise you do, the more likely a person is to increase his or her ability to resist temptations and to show greater perseverance with any other task at hand. The benefits are so profound that they will create a rippling effect of all round goodness in your life, in terms of attaining goals and making those dreams turn into reality. So what are you waiting for? Begin a daily workout today. Make a commitment to yourself, first and foremost, to turn up for forty days. It's easier when you have a short term date to work towards. Forty days of new behaviour actually determines a pathway in your brain to form a habit. If you form a habit of daily exercise, you are definitely on the way to success in all other areas of your life inshaAllah!

The book *Spark! How exercise will improve the performance of your brain* highlights a revolutionary method of fitness, adopted by a professor at a school in Chicago, on a group of students. They began each day with a run, where they timed themselves and measured their heart rates. The idea was to get their heart rates above 185 and then try to beat their own time every day. The professor Neil Duncan says, of the method, 'What we're really doing is trying to get them prepared to learn, through rigorous exercise.' He found that as well as improving the students' mood at school, the literacy level was boosted through improved reading and comprehension scores. It's a huge lesson to learn. If one needs to boost the output of the mind, increase the oxygen levels to the brain via a good bout of exercise and witness the innumerable benefits. If you're looking for something to 'supercharge your thinking, beat stress, reverse ageing, fight memory loss, lift your mood, sharpen your intellect', then look no further than making a plan to get some regular exercise into your life. And rejoice in the fact that being somebody who exercises every day, makes you one of the healthiest people on the planet (no matter your size or shape!).

If, like me, you're accustomed to seeking out sweet treats or lots of carbs as comfort food when you're stressed or looking to give yourself some self-care, you'll do well to remind yourself that it's a cycle worth getting out of. If you change the response to that trigger, for example, turn to exercise instead, the inevitable sugar low that you will experience as an after-effect of eating the wrong foods will be non-existent, and you'll experience the benefits of a natural mood enhancer and stress buster to boot. Clearing mind-fog, feeling great and looking good are also fantastic side benefits. What have you got to lose?

It's so important to be consistent with exercise. Set a small goal, for example, an exercise class a week, and stick to it. Build it up from there. Slot in a few minutes of exercise in your day, even if it's getting up every hour (if you tend to sit down at your day job) and walking around. Hey, how about buying yourself a pedometer? You can easily download an app that does the same thing (although, I'd be wary of carrying my phone with me everywhere I go simply to count steps). You'll be amazed at how much your activity increases once you know it's being counted! It's actually been proven that those who wear a pedometer will walk more. It helps you to become more mindful of your daily activity. Take the bus or train instead of the car every once in a while. Be aware of how good movement is for your health and well-being. It's amazing how much a few minutes of exercise can affect your stress and energy levels. It's incredible, really. A huge blessing from Allah ﷻ. Top it off with the fact that the feel-good chemical, endorphins, are released into your blood after a good workout and this is enough to get you up and going again.

The biggest mistake people make is to sign up to too much too soon, and then they end up suffering with burnout which means they don't get to see the long-term benefits. Set a small sustainable goal and stick to it and then build it up from there. Every good act begins with a small, bite-sized commitment.

I've known some people to give themselves a small treat at the end of a day, as a tangible reward for all the abstention. Others still, have a 'cheat' day which means they can eat whatever they want guilt-free for one day of the week. If this idea of 'cheating' or feeding yourself the foods you want to avoid in order to be healthy doesn't sit right with you, then maybe you can take a day where you eat out or eat at a family member or friend's house without worrying too much about the nutritional value. I'm saying this because I have seen many people go through diets and various eating programmes and the ones that seem to maintain their healthy eating for the longest are the ones that allow themselves a little leeway in the form of treats. I remember someone looking at me in disapproval and indignation as I drank a sugary soft drink whilst on a 'healthy eating programme', and had I let it affect me or my thinking I might have thrown the towel in and agreed that I wasn't playing the game right. I reminded myself how good I'd been all week and I managed to continue on the path I had begun. That is the main goal. To continue, no matter what. Thankfully, I can report that during that particular bout I stayed on track and managed to lose a significant amount of weight.

I've got to admit that sometimes, even when I have started to become more aware of what I'm doing to my body and have begun to make a change, I sometimes fall off the bandwagon. The secret, after the lapse, is to continue and not to give up. We all have moments of weakness—the worst thing to do at this point is to write off the whole day or (God forbid!) the week, month or even the whole idea. If you continue with your goal, regardless of your inability to be strict about everything, you really will get somewhere. And hopefully, reaching your mini-goals will be the fuel to help you continue long enough to reach your long-term goals.

When you feel that your will is weakening and you're not sure if you can carry on, one of the things you can do is seek out someone who has reached the goals you are striving to achieve and speak to them to strengthen your resolve and carry on. You can train your willpower so that you can rely on it and it becomes very strong, but you need to start with baby steps. Interestingly, waking up for *Fajr* plays a part in this. It increases our willpower and determination in all other areas of our lives. This is a miracle of this prayer and no doubt, there are also many more! Begin training your willpower by breaking up the tasks you want to perform into smaller tasks, and tackle them one at a time. Build it up slowly and you'll see, that it will increase. People will wonder where you get the willpower and drive to succeed from, and it'll be your little secret. You will have trained it, like any other muscle, subhanAllah.

Remain active, whatever you do and when you feel your weight climbing up, nip it in the bud so it can't get the better of you!

How Do You Get Started?

If you are happy with your weight, then your diet probably doesn't need to change much. Lower your carb and sugar intake, eat more greens, good fats and work on clearing out your gut flora. Drinking kefir or a probiotic drink regularly will help with this. To maintain your weight, aim for three bouts of thirty minutes of exercise per week.

If you are not happy with your weight, be mindful of what you eat and begin with lessening your portion size. Keep a food diary if you're unsure as to why you can't maintain a good weight. Think of how well clothes fit you, rather than focusing on your weight, as weight can fluctuate a lot (for lots of reasons). Use a tape measure (or even a piece of string) to measure your waistline, and rejoice when it becomes smaller! Aim for five or more thirty minute bouts of exercise per week to lose weight. It usually works better to do this on the weekdays and rest on the weekend.

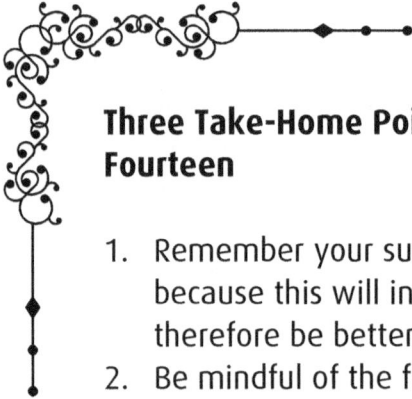

Three Take-Home Points for Chapter Fourteen

1. Remember your sunnahs when eating because this will increase the blessings and therefore be better for your health.
2. Be mindful of the food that you are eating. More often than not, if one is taking care of their inside, their outside glows with health and one naturally looks their best.
3. Exercising regularly helps flush toxins from the body and makes one look and feel their best. Buddy up with a support group to keep going. Best of luck.

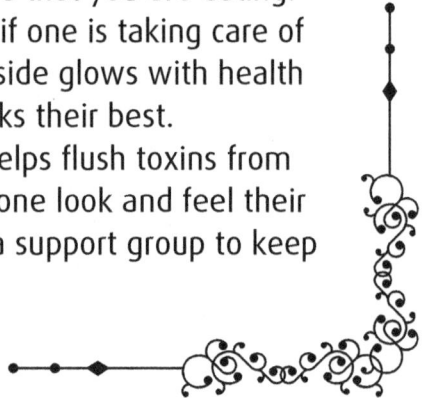

I hope this discussion about healthy eating and exercise inspires you to get up and move! Now onto making sure you get a good night's sleep.

Chapter Fifteen

On Sleep and Stillness

What Happens If I Don't Prioritise Sleep?

Everyone has experienced the fatigue, short temper and lack of focus that often follows a poor night's sleep. An occasional night without sleep makes you feel tired and irritable the next day, but it won't harm your health.

After several sleepless nights, the mental effects become more serious. Your brain will fog, making it difficult to concentrate and make decisions. You'll start to feel down, and may fall asleep during the day. Your risk of injury and accidents at home, work and on the road increases too.

If it continues, lack of sleep can affect your overall health and make you prone to serious medical conditions, such as obesity, heart disease, high blood pressure and diabetes. Here are some reasons why it is imperative to get a good amount of sleep every night (at least 7-8 hours) and how it will help to boost your overall health:

1. **Sleep boosts immunity.** If you seem to catch every cold and flu that's going around, your bedtime could be to blame. Prolonged lack of sleep can disrupt your immune system, so you're less able to fend off bugs.

2. **Sleep can slim you.** Sleeping less may mean you put on weight! Studies have shown that people who sleep less than seven hours a day tend to gain more weight and have a higher risk of becoming obese than those who get seven hours or more of slumber. It's believed to be because sleep-deprived people have reduced levels of leptin (the chemical that makes you feel full) and increased levels of ghrelin (the hunger-stimulating hormone).

3. **Sleep boosts mental wellbeing.** Given that a single sleep-less night can make you irritable and moody the following day, it's not surprising that chronic sleep debt may lead to long-term mood disorders like depression and anxiety. When people with anxiety or depression were surveyed to calculate their sleeping habits, it turned out that most of them slept for less than six hours a night.

4. **Sleep increases sex drive.** Men and women who don't get enough quality sleep have lower libidos and less of an interest in sex. Research shows men who suffer from sleep apnoea—a disorder in which breathing difficulties lead to interrupted sleep—also tend to have lower testosterone levels, which can lower libido.

5. **Sleep increases fertility.** Difficulty conceiving a baby has been claimed as one of the effects of sleep deprivation, in both men and women. Apparently, regular sleep disruptions can cause trouble conceiving by reducing the secretion of reproductive hormones (Source: NHS website). It is imperative that we look after ourselves and make sure we have enough sleep each night to function properly the next day. This fascinating information and more has been studied at Harvard University.

Here are some tips to improve your quality of sleep:

- Be aware of the effects of stimulants. Avoid caffeinated beverages (coffee, many teas, chocolate, and some soft drinks) after 1 or 2pm, or altogether, if you're especially caffeine-sensitive. Caffeine blocks the effects of adenosine, a brain chemical thought to promote sleep.

- Maybe you could take a 15 to 20 minute nap just after noon-time—that's usually long enough to improve alertness but not so long that you feel groggy afterward. Don't nap at all in the evening. Of course, this is part of the Prophetic sunnah too. How wonderful to witness that modern science promotes this.

- Exercise. Yes! Exercise features once again. It's so important to get regular aerobic exercise such as walking, jogging, or swimming, which can help you fall asleep faster, get deeper sleep, and awaken less often during the night.

- Build strong habits. A regular sleep routine helps synchronise your sleep/wake cycle. Once you determine how much time in bed you need, go to bed each night and get up each morning at the same time. As human beings we love routines! Establishing good habits will help maintain success on this front in the long run.

- Make your bedroom a peaceful sanctuary. Reserve it for sleep, intimacy, and restful activities such as meditation and reading for pleasure. Make sure your mattress and pillow is comfortable. Keep it cool, dark, and quiet at night. To block out noises, consider using a fan or another appliance that produces a steady 'white noise'. You can use apps with white noise on them—although I wouldn't recommend having a mobile phone turned on and close by while you are sleeping because of the effects of radiation. White noise is proven to help babies sleep and in fact, I used it for my youngest child in the early months of his life. Initially it didn't sit right with me. Why put on 'white noise' when you can put on the wonderful soothing intonations of the Quran? But whilst researching, I found out that the white noise actually simulates the sound that the baby hears whilst in the mother's womb. The *Lutf*, the gentle subtle care, in which Allah, the Most High, keeps us safe and protected within the mother's womb is replicated via this sound. And that's how I made my peace with it. Alhamdulillah.

- Eat mindfully. Finish dinner several hours before bedtime. If you need a snack in the evening, eat a small serving of something you know won't disturb your digestion, such as yoghurt, cereal and milk, or a piece of buttered toast.

- Put your phone away. Research has shown that the glare of the phone screen will negatively affect your ability to fall asleep and even the quality of sleep that you get.

- Don't keep checking the time. Watching the sleepless minutes pass makes it harder to fall back to sleep in the early hours of the morning.

- Establish a relaxing routine before bedtime. Consider meditation, a warm shower or some simple stretches to loosen muscles. Maybe you'd like to save your evening *witr* to pray just before bedtime. Avoid things that might cause stress, such as work or emotional discussions.

- Limit drinks before bedtime, especially the aforementioned caffeine. To minimise nighttime trips to the bathroom, try not to drink anything during the two or three hours before bedtime.

Sleeping With a Baby

I highly recommend the book *Three in a Bed* by Deborah Jackson. The author discusses the fact that only since the Victorian times has it been standard practice for mothers and fathers to send their babies to sleep alone, away from the parental bed, often in another room. This book reveals how babies who sleep with their parents benefit by getting virtually a full night's sleep. The author explains the advantages of this 'radical' form of baby care, including its benefits for breastfeeding mothers. She then reviews the history of keeping babies in the bed via studies of different cultures around the world and, through interviews with parents, explores contemporary attitudes to the idea. The book also contains a fresh perspective on the tragedy of cot death, as well as practical advice on how to sustain your sex life, hints on safety in the bed and answers to all the common objections. Finally, the author deals with the moment when the baby leaves the parents' bed.

The idea that co-sleeping is inherently dangerous for babies is an urban myth. Generations of parents have been made to feel guilty if they cuddle up to their children at night, even though they may get more sleep; breastfeeding is easier; crying rates are drastically reduced; babies breathe more steadily; sleep hormones are stimulated; baby's core temperature is regulated by skin-to-skin contact; parental confidence is boosted and it becomes possible to react swiftly in a crisis. We feel guilty even though cot death is unheard of in cot-less cultures in Africa to Asia and South America, while thousands of American and some 200 British babies still die every year from Sudden Infant Death Syndrome (SIDs).

Needless to say, I totally believe that not only is it safe to sleep with one's baby, it's a must if you both want to get a full night's sleep, not to mention the other numerous astounding benefits.

On Stillness

Not only does somebody who chooses to remain silent avoid conflict but sitting in silence generally also has many other physical and mental health benefits.

Alhamdulillah, as a family, we were very blessed to have visited many beautiful sights in the UK this summer. I've got to admit that silence for us whilst outdoors facilitated listening out for nature and the innumerable glorious signs of Allah ﷻ on the earth. To be silent and reflect whilst at sea, looking out at a beautiful coastline and backdrop of hazy mountains in the distance, deepens one's imaan and gratitude to the Creator for such natural beauty in the world. The heart constricts with wonder and awe and one can't help think of the ayah in our glorious Quran which states:

> 'Our Lord! Not for naught hast Thou created (all) this!
> Glory be to Thee!'
> [Quran 3:191]

I definitely think that this is a vital aspect of our lives that is missing right now. We might not reap the same benefits whilst sitting in silence, in our concrete jungles of towns and cities but every now and again, sitting quietly maybe whilst reading the Quran or doing some silent dhikr will certainly deepen one's feeling of peace and tranquility and will aid such reflection that will help us to remember why we're here in the first place. I highly recommend making regular slots of quietness and solitude in your daily and weekly routines inshaAllah.

Not only will this silence help you to maintain a close relationship with Allah ﷻ but it will also help you to put any negative feelings you have towards anybody into perspective (supplementing what we have already learnt in Chapter Seven).

Let's use this moment to take a look at some other benefits of silence:

- Improving memory
- Stimulating brain growth
- In a recent study, scientists found that when mice were exposed to two hours of silence per day, they developed cells in the hippocampus region of the brain. This region is connected to memory, emotion and learning. SubhanAllah.
- Relieving stress
- Fighting insomnia
- Heightening sensitivity

Silence is hugely beneficial in so many ways. Whoever thought there'd be so many benefits to remaining silent? InshaAllah it will remind us all to choose to remain silent more often. A huge reason also to turn off those notifications and go back to the phone serving us rather than the other way round (as mentioned in Chapter Thirteen). Let's try to silence ourselves a little more. Let's go for substance over frivolous comments and see how much time it frees up! Even better would be to silence ourselves by turning off the phones and concentrating on the present.

Waking Up Just Before Dawn

Apparently it's quite a common phenomenon as one gets older, to spontaneously wake up in the early hours every morning. I know somebody very wise who studies Arabic at this precise time every day. Wow. I know. It is a time for quiet solitude, reflection and a special time for connectedness with your Creator. As we know, God doesn't exist in 'time' and 'space', rather He is the Creator of these things. This time is when He descends to the lowermost heaven and says, 'Who is calling Me, so that

I may answer him? Who is asking Me so that I may grant him? Who is seeking forgiveness from Me so that I may forgive him?'

There are two ways to interpret this saying. These are:

1. His mercy, command and angels descend (just as we can say in English 'the King made this town', i.e. he commissioned for the town to be made, though the workers were the ones who actually did the job).
2. It is a metaphor for His gentleness to those making supplication (i.e. at that time of night) and His answering them.

It is reported that the Messenger ﷺ was asked, 'What prayer is most virtuous, after the five daily prayers?' He said, 'Prayer in the depths of the night.'

Night prayer is superior to day prayer because it is more concealed and closer to sincerity. The early Muslims used to strive hard to hide their secrets (meaning the actions between them and God). A well-known wise man Hassan al-Basri said, 'It used to be that a person would have guests staying over and he would pray at night without his guests knowing.'

Night prayer is harder on the lower self or ego, because night is a time of rest, so leaving sleep despite the lower self being desirous of it is a tremendous struggle. Some have said, 'The best of works are those the lower self is forced to perform.' So, stamp on that nafs (ego) and force yourself to increase in spiritual works, especially when it seems hard! Remember, the way to Paradise is surrounded by difficulty and the way to hellfire is surrounded by ease, so choose carefully how you spend your time! As always, this is a reminder for me, first and foremost.

Recitation in night prayer is closer to contemplation, because things that usually busy the heart in the daytime are mostly absent at night, so the heart is at attention and is with the tongue in understanding.

Night vigil time is the best of times for voluntary worship and prayer, and the closest a servant is to his Lord. It is a time when the doors of the sky are opened, supplications are answered, and the needs of those who ask are fulfilled.

Use this time to be mindfully still. Engage in the art of stopping to wonder, to thank, to contemplate, to supplicate and reflect. Let your heart be still in remembrance of the Creator. Let it be still while others are asleep. Let it be still from its needs and wants. Let it be still and take in the reality of why we are here and where we are headed. Let your heart be still and nourish your soul with His food.

The Almighty has praised those who wake up at night for His remembrance, supplication, and to seek forgiveness and entreat Him, saying:

> 'They forsake their beds to cry unto their Lord in fear
> and hope, and spend of what We have bestowed on
> them. No soul knows what is kept hidden from them of
> joy, as a reward for what they used to do.'
> [Quran 32:16-17]

The upshot is that there are many, many reasons why a full night's sleep, around eight hours, is important for the body and mind. However, if you do find yourself awake in the middle of the night don't stress. Use this unique beautiful time for reflection and feed your soul, and make up for the lost time in a sunnah afternoon nap. As Rumi said:

> 'The breezes at dawn have secrets to tell you
> Don't go back to sleep!
> You must ask for what you really want.
> Don't go back to sleep!

People are going back and forth
across the doorsill where the two worlds touch,
The door is round and open
Don't go back to sleep!'
[Rumi]

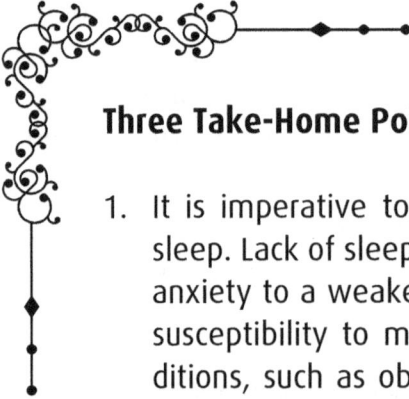

Three Take-Home Points for Chapter Fifteen

1. It is imperative to prioritise a good night's sleep. Lack of sleep can cause ill effects from anxiety to a weakened immune system and susceptibility to many serious medical conditions, such as obesity, heart disease, high blood pressure and diabetes.

2. Babies who sleep with their parents benefit by getting a full night's sleep.

3. Sleep early and wake in the last part of the night for worship. Night vigil time is the best of times for voluntary worship and prayer, and the closest a servant is to his Lord. Use this time to be mindfully still. Engage in the art of stopping to wonder, to thank, to contemplate, to supplicate and reflect. Let your heart be still in remembrance of the Creator.

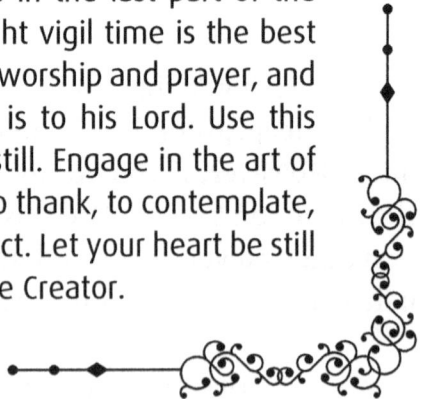

Chapter Sixteen
On Contentment

Many times in our lives when we feel things are going wrong and there seems to be no barakah in our actions, then take heed and turn back to Allah, the Most High. Allah ﷻ is calling you to return to Him by reminding you that there is no tranquility in the heart, mind or soul without the remembrance of Him. Through the remembrance of Him, heedlessness leaves us, we remember our purpose and the barakah returns inshaAllah.

'Verily in the remembrance of Allah do hearts find rest.'
[Quran 13:28]

As one of my beloved teachers once mentioned, when we are young, we wish to be older. When we are old enough, we wish for a decent job, and we make this our dhikr or remembrance. Then, maybe we'll wish for a spouse and make this our dhikr. Then, comes a desire for children, for wealth, great holidays, a big home, a brand new car and later on, even grandchildren. The list can be endless. Our dhikr is worldly, confusing and can never make us content.

We expect life to follow a logical pattern, an order, a path that society has mapped out for us. But life isn't like that and then we complain, we lose hope and some even fall into despair.

Who are these complainers? Those who always look at what's wrong in their lives? They are those who are competitive and never content and grateful for what they have. Their discontent with themselves and their lives runs too deep. But we know that Allah ﷻ loves those who return often to Him. And it can never be too late to turn things around.

I'm going to invite you to step out of the box so we can change the narrative together.

Instead of looking at what we haven't got, we need to look in the other direction. Let's look at what we have got, as discussed previously in the chapter on Gratitude. And then within our religion, we must always look to people who have more spirituality than ourselves and strive to be better. We must swap things around so that we are happy with less materialism and are always striving for more spirituality in our lives!

As one of my beloved teachers said, rather than all these worldly pursuits, if we make our dhikr and remembrance Allah ﷻ from the outset then everything will fall into place. There will be no flitting about, trying to attain more and more duniya, there will be no restlessness—only peace.

To find contentment in the moment as it is passing is truly a great blessing. Contentment with the will of Allah ﷻ, with whatever He has destined, knowing that your life has been planned and written over hundreds of thousands of years ago by the Greatest of Writers, knowing that if you were given a choice, seeing the future, and choosing the best path for yourself, you would also choose the exact same way, the exact same path, is a very rare and huge gift indeed.

Allah ﷻ, through His Divine Love and Mercy contrives matters such that you reach your own potential throughout your personal, unique trials and struggles. It's a battle you cannot lose, if you keep sight of your goal, which is closeness to Allah in this life and the hereafter.

'Allah does not burden a soul beyond that which it can bear.'
[Quran 2:286]

This is a promise that Allah ﷻ makes to us and through which we are given hope and strength to remain positive through hardship.

Make sure that, if everything else falls apart, Allah, the Most High, is enough for you and He will take care of your duniya. Make Him, just Him, your focus and everything else will fall into place inshaAllah.

'And He is with you, wherever you are.'
[Quran 57:4]

It's not wrong to want beautiful things. Allah, the Most High, is Beautiful and loves beauty in His creation mashaAllah. We are told to keep ourselves looking clean and pleasant and it is totally OK ladies, in a halal environment to beautify yourselves for each other.

It's not wrong either, to want a comfortable life, but when your desires for this duniya surpass your desire to please your Creator, then you need to stop and think about what you're doing.

It isn't worldly to want more in order to become a stronger, better believer, or in order to free yourself up so you can use up your time for a more noble cause.

But it is imperative to know that fulfilment will never lie in worldly gains. The thing we have to be the wariest of is holding the duniya in our hearts and not our hands. Once, I heard of a relief worker who helped with the biggest Tsunami of 2004 say he'd never seen so many *awliya,* or friends of Allah ﷻ, in one place. Their contentment with the will of Allah surpassed no other. They had lost their homes, families, jobs and suffered many unspeakable losses, but those who kept Allah in their hearts were victorious. As one of my teachers once told us, 'A Sufi flourishes in adversity.' What a glorious example to behold!

On the other hand, many a millionaire has died with the depressing reality that money does not equal happiness. You only have to look at the world of celebrities and their divorce and suicide rates to come to the conclusion that monetary gain is not as fulfilling as people would have us believe.

We were once told a story, by the wise Shaykh Mohammed Aslam, of Birmingham. He told us of a world famous chef who would work for celebrities. He'd go into their houses and cook for them. He spoke of how much discontentment and disarray he found in these places. In contrast, he was asked to work in a poor part of a Muslim land and he was astonished at how little they had and how great their happiness was. He was so taken aback that he converted to Islam. SubhanAllah!

Happiness lies in communities, in support, in love for one another and first and foremost, in the remembrance of our Creator, the Most High. The 'small things' are underrated. They are in fact 'big things'. If only we stopped to take stock of the blessings right under our noses, Allah, the Most High, has promised us they will be increased, if only we were aware of the true nature of such gems. We would be shown that these are the most important and the ones that matter the most. Everything else is simply a bonus.

Have passions, aspirations, reach for your best self and strive to become a beacon of light for those around you. This is a part of the Prophetic example; wanting for others what you want for yourself—true altruism. Ours is a social deen. Our men are asked to take an active part in the community (at least) every week for Jummah. Our worldly cares are tied strongly to our religious obligations. Contentment in our everyday lives does not mean we cannot strive for change. We can and we should. The Prophet ﷺ said:

> 'Allah the Most High said, "I am as My servant thinks
> (expects) I am. I am with him when he mentions Me.
> If he mentions Me to himself, I mention him to Myself;
> and if he mentions Me in an assembly, I mention him in
> an assembly greater than it. If he draws near to Me a
> hand's length, I draw near to him an arm's length. And
> if he comes to Me walking, I go to him at speed."'
> [Bukhari]

Commentary:

> 'I am as my slave expects Me to be':
> Ibn Hajar (may Allah have Mercy upon him) said:
> 'meaning, I am able to do whatever he expects I will do.'
> [Fath al-Bari]

If we believe that we will be looked after in this life and Allah will reward us for any good intentions we may have and be with us through thick and thin, then by the truth of Allah's words, we will have 'what we expect'. Always have a good opinion of Allah. He will manifest it as the truth inshaAllah.

If you begin every task with *Bismillah*, Allah ﷻ will put barakah in it inshaAllah. If you strive hard for the deen with a sincere intention and work hard in the duniya with honesty and a noble aim, then both the deen and duniya will fall into your lap, by the Mercy of Allah. Don't despair, have a good opinion of Allah, and He will fulfil it for you. His Mercy and Love is there for the taking, if only we focus on what is important in life.

> 'And whoever puts all his trust in Allah,
> He will be enough for him.'
> [Quran 65:1]

May Allah, the Most High, bring the reality of the akhira closer to us, so that we are aware of how lofty and high our simple acts of devotion will be in the next life and we intend closeness though each one.

Speaking of intentions, my beloved teacher taught us that we can intend everything for the sake of Allah ﷻ in one sweep. Lest you are deprived of rewards through the mindlessness of fulfilling your duties in this life through ritual habits and mind-numbing activities, this is a wonderful secret to attain reward for every second spent on this earth and make it work in your favour in the akhira inshaAllah. And here it is:

Intend every breath, every thought and every action you take for the sake of Allah *right now*. May it all be written as never-ending goodness for you! May Allah, the Most High, help us to remain content in the here and now, recognising each minute blessing and showing gratefulness through obedience and love always, inshaAllah. Ameen.

Three Take-Home Points for Chapter Sixteen

1. *'Verily in the remembrance of Allah do hearts find rest.'* [Quran 13:28]
2. Let's be grateful for everything we have been given in this duniya, by looking at those who have less than us. In our deen, we must always look to people who have more than ourselves and strive to be better.
3. If you strive hard for the deen with a sincere intention and work hard in the duniya with honesty and a noble aim, then both the deen and duniya will fall into your lap, by the Mercy of Allah. Don't despair, have a good opinion of Allah, and He will fulfil it for you.

Epilogue
Trust in Allah

*'So when the Quran is recited, listen to it and pay
attention that you may receive Mercy.'*
[Quran 7:204]

Whenever things start to get too much in life, pick up the Quran and read. Read a translation or a commentary and maybe begin to learn Arabic in order for you to make sense of it yourself. I have come across a fantastic app called *Duolingo* and it is really great for beginners and intermediate learners of the Arabic language. Download it today—maybe you'll see my name with yours on the scoreboard one day! You could also consider learning the majestic meaning of our Holy Book on a tafseer course. It is well-known that Arabic is one of the most difficult and complex languages to learn in the world. The depth of layers in meaning is unimaginable and even then the prose is still very powerful (most of the Quran reads like an invitation to believe, one of the most famous lines from surah *Ar-Rahman* The Merciful reads 'Which of Allah's favours can you deny?'), it doesn't come across in the translation. It definitely requires an in-depth study to fully understand the complete message that was left for us.

Otherwise there are many benefits of simply reading the Quran in Arabic and these days there is no shortage of reciters. There was a time when one would have to travel to Mecca to find a decent full recitation of the Quran on CD; nowadays you can simply type in a surah on YouTube and sit back and listen. Many come with a translation, the Arabic script and even transliteration if required. The information age can be very useful to us if used to do good!

Our last and final Messenger Muhammad ﷺ preached to the people to trust in Allah ﷻ, the Most High. When we study his life and the decisions he made, there are many examples of the firmness of his belief and in this is a great reminder for us all. His life story, or seerah, can be read and studied from many books.

There are many examples in the seerah that show the Prophet's immense trust in God. However great the danger that confronted him, he never lost hope and never allowed himself to be worried or agitated. His uncle Abu Talib knew the feelings of the Quraysh (the name of his family's tribe, who mostly opposed the message of One God) when the Prophet ﷺ started his mission. He also knew the lengths to which the Quraysh would go to stop him, and requested the Prophet ﷺ to abandon his mission. The Prophet ﷺ replied:

> 'Dear Uncle, do not judge this situation by my
> loneliness. Truth will not go unsupported for long.
> The whole of Arabia and beyond will one day
> support its cause.'
> [Ibn Hisham]

When the attitude of the Quraysh became more threatening, Abu Talib again begged his nephew to renounce his mission but the Prophet's ﷺ reply was:

'O my Uncle, if they placed the sun in my right hand and the moon in my left, to force me to renounce my work, verily I would not desist therefrom until Allah made manifest His cause, or I perished in the attempt.'
[Ibid]

The immense trust in Allah ﷻ overpowered any feeling to obtain material gains in this duniya. Another time, his best friend and dear companion, Abu Bakr (may Allah be pleased with him) was frightened when pursuers came close to the cave in which he and Prophet Muhammad ﷺ were hiding during their flight from Mecca to Medina, but the Prophet ﷺ reassured him, 'Grieve not. Allah is with us.'

A guard was kept at the Prophet's house in Medina because of the danger that surrounded him but he had him withdrawn when the Quranic verse was revealed:

'Allah will protect you from the people.'
[Quran 5:67]

Throughout each and every trial and tribulation of his life, complete faith and trust in the Almighty appears as the dominant feature. It is a great example for us to follow.

'Remember Allah during times of ease and He will remember you during times of difficulty.'
[Tirmidhi]

Never despair. Allah's door is always open. And the doors of Mercy and His Forgiveness will remain open until our last breath.

Allah says in a beautiful hadith:

'O son of Adam, so long as you call upon Me and ask of Me, I shall forgive you for what you have done, and I shall not mind. O son of Adam, were your sins to reach the clouds of the sky and were you then to ask forgiveness of Me, I would forgive you. O son of Adam, were you to come to Me with sins nearly as great as the earth and were you then to face Me, ascribing no partner to Me, I would bring you forgiveness nearly as great as it.'
[Tirmidhi]

In this life, there will be no regrets—only a chance to learn from our mistakes, but in the next life the greatest regret will be that we didn't worship Allah ﷻ to a greater capacity. May Allah ﷻ help us to remember Him always and trust in Him to do what's best for us, for He is Most Merciful.

Don't forget that when it comes to any trauma that we have faced, or anything which we are indeed continuously facing in life, remember that it is still we who decide how it affects us. It isn't the event, but rather the emotions we attach to the event that can threaten to unravel us. As mentioned earlier, we can choose whether we want to be Worriers or Warriors! May Allah ﷻ help us through all adversities in the best way. Remind yourself that those closest and most beloved to Allah are tried and tested the most.

'If we had perfect power to determine our destinies, and perfect vision to see the future and know what is best for us, we would choose exactly the fate that Allah has chosen for us.'
[Imam al-Ghazali]

*'If we knew how meticulously Allah ﷻ plans our affairs
for us, our hearts would break out of love for Him.'*
[Imam Shafi'i]

It's strange to know that many people who are successful in this world actually come from a very testing background. They manage to turn their lives around for the better and through sharing their stories, have encouraged others to do the same and then, these examples are echoed around the world. Many famous people have undergone enormous change and improvement from living and working through a difficult circumstance in life. They have used their difficulty and heartache to propel themselves further and have therefore maximised their capacity for good and honest work. Some of them will admit that their horrendous, frightening and seemingly unfair past is a part of their story. It's part of who they are today and surprisingly, most wouldn't change it. Going through those life-changing events has made them stronger.

*'Imagine this scenario. Your mother comes to your
house and tells you she'd like to take you out and to get
into the car. During the journey, you notice the roads
are unfamiliar and bumpy. It is getting dark and you
are in unfamiliar territory and you're not sure where
you are heading. Are you going to panic? No. You would
not panic for one simple reason. You trust the driver.
Now, think about who is "driving" our lives. When you
are going through a rough time, you have to ask yourself one simple question: Do you trust the Driver?'*
[Anon]

Allah ﷻ knows the wisdom behind certain events in our lives; suffice to say that He is Just, He loves us as no human being ever could and He sent Messengers to guide us onto the straight path. Through true *tawakkul* we forego worry and hardship. We find peace through prayer and love.

May we live to be strong human beings with fortitude of character, Love of the Divine and of those who see the Prophet Muhammad's ﷺ example of compassion towards one another, forbearance and trust as the best example and live by it as much as we can, ameen.

Life is not always easy or full of light and happiness but know that we can only do the best with the tools that we are given and the capacity that we have. I wish you all the best in life!

'Now there's no need to be perfect, you can be good!'
[Anon]

Nobody expects perfection! Allah ﷻ knows how many times I've worked on this book and thought, who on earth am I to write a self-development book on life? What gives me the authority? I am the first one to admit that I'm not perfect and I don't have the solution to every problem. All I can say is that Allah ﷻ inspired me to write to you and here I am and now that it is done, I feel a huge relief that the voices in my head have been quietened (for now!).

Remember that there is always someone who cares, if you look hard enough.

Peace and love,

Sidra Ansari

Three Take-Home Points for the Epilogue

1. Stay close to Allah and His beloved Messenger through the Quran and Sunnah during the good times and the trials of life. Through translations of the Quran and contemplation on what our beloved Messenger went through in his blessed life there are many examples to draw upon.
2. 'Remember Allah during times of ease and He will remember you during times of difficulty.'(Tirmidhi)
3. Through true *tawakkul* we forego worry and hardship. We find peace through prayer and love.

Recommended Reading

Chapter Five

- *Enough* by John Naish

Chapter Six

On Marriage:

As it is nearly impossible to cover every aspect of this hot topic, I recommend that you read around the subject. A lot. Books I recommend are:

- *Men Are from Mars, Women Are from Venus: A Practical Guide for Improving Communication and Getting What You Want in Your Relationships* by John Gray
- *Fascinating Womanhood* by Helen Andelin
- *Surrendered Wife* by Laura Doyle
- *Initiating and Upholding an Islamic Marriage* by Hedaya Hartford
- *The Five Love Languages* by Dr. Gary Chapman

To take a quiz to find out your own love language visit: *www.5lovelanguages.com/quizzes/*

There are also a few courses I highly recommend: Anything to do with Laura Doyle and her book, *Surrendered Wife*; she has a website where you can sign up to learning more.

At the time of writing, there are three sources I would recommend: Sara Malik's fabulous website, cherishedandsuccessful.com and check out her coaching or the highly inspirational Naielah Ackbarali at her website, *Muslimacoaching* (formerly named tayyibaatwives.com). Naielah has been trained personally by Laura Doyle herself. Lastly and most notably, the aforementioned teacher, Ustadha Hedaya Hartford who has recently teamed up with Dr. Ayiesha Malik at *muslimmarriagelife-coaching.com.* They have joined forces to help with Life Coaching and specialising in marriage in particular. All four teachers are highly professional and wonderfully compassionate and understanding.

Chapter Eight

- *Islamic Manners* by Shaykh Abdal-Fattah Abu Ghuddah
- Faber and Mazlish's *How to Talk So Kids Will Listen & Listen So Kids Will Talk'*
- *The Book You Wish Your Parents Had Read (and Your Children Will Be Glad That You Did)* by Phillipa Perry
- *Slow and Steady Get Me Ready* by June Oberunner
- *The Ordinary Parent's Guide to Teaching Reading* by Susan and Jessie Wise
- A set (or two) of levelled reading books
- *Singapore Maths Workbooks and Textbooks* (incidentally these are becoming popular in state schools due to the importance now given to children learning through concrete aspects rather than sticking to the abstract). Also, see *whiterosemaths.com.*

Chapter Twelve

- *Sea Without Shore* by Nuh Ha Meem Keller

For those of you who are new to Sufism, I thoroughly recommend this practical guide and manual. There is simply nothing out there in the English language quite as all-encompassing as this extremely meticulously researched book. The first half of the book is more of a light and enjoyable read as Shaikh Nuh regales us with tales of Sufi past. Memorable, humorous and not to be missed.

Chapter Fourteen

I'm going to list the books that have helped me to understand how to listen to my body and choose the right eating pattern for me.

- *Lean For Life: Transform your body in 6 weeks, Protect the results forever* by Louise Parker
- *Wheat Belly Total Health* by William Davis
- *Not on the Label* by Felicity Lawrence
- *Lean for Life; The Louise Parker Method* by Louise Parker
- *Spark! How exercise will improve the performance of your brain* by Neil Duncan

Chapter Sixteen

On Seerah or the Life of the Prophet ﷺ

My favourite lessons are a commentary by Shaykh Hamza Yusuf on the book *Muhammad: His Life Based on the Earliest Sources* by Martin Lings. The book is available on Audible and the commentary can be bought in a CD set and even found on YouTube. It is a thoroughly heart-warming and comforting series of lessons which suffice in the student finding out so much about the Prophet ﷺ that they attain a closeness. The Shaikh is a former nurse and very articulate in presenting the vast dimensions of his knowledge, which he obtained in the deserts of Mauritania, to the class. He is the president, co-founder and senior faculty member of Zaytuna College in California.

Endnote

If you would like to obtain sacred knowledge or find out more about Traditional Islam, I would recommend *Seekershub. org*, which, at the time of writing, is a fantastic online organisation begun in Toronto which has actually gathered together many, many contemporary scholars who are voluntarily teaching thousands upon thousands of national and international students true Islamic Knowledge every single year! It's an impressive feat. Not only do they serve the masses in terms of education, they also give fatwas (search the tab 'Answers' on the website) that are relevant to this day and age and do not 'water down' Islam, which is a common practice these days. Islam was sent down as a message to the whole of Humanity until the End of Time, therefore even though not all the rulings apply, most of them cannot be compromised. Any present day questions one might have are answered in a wonderfully practical and down-to-earth manner which I've found to be immensely helpful. Their website is a fountain of knowledge—and long may it continue! Here, I'd like to remind you that if you want to learn about the true nature of Islam, do not simply use Google to ask questions. There are many laymen starting blogs and answering questions without the knowledge or authority to do so and this can have awful consequences. Make sure you check your sources! Websites like *Seekershub.org* help so much as the onus is not on you to verify your facts.

Acknowledgements

First of all, I'd like to praise Allah, Al-Kareem, for every-thing. My gratitude transcends the heavens and the earth and only Allah ﷻ knows how indebted I am to His Lutf in my life. Alhamdulillah.

'And He found you lost and guided [you].'
[Quran 93:7]

I would like to praise our Beloved Rasul ﷺ who inspired me to use the name Ansari for on the day of the Conquest of Mecca, when the Prophet had given the Muhajiroon (the Quraysh who had travelled from Makkah to Medina) the spoils of war (the booty), the Ansar said: 'By Allah, this is indeed very strange: While our swords are still dripping with the blood of Quraysh, our war booty is distributed amongst them.'

When this news reached the Prophet he called the Ansar and said, 'What is this news that has reached me from you?'

They replied, 'What has reached you is true.'

He said, 'Doesn't it please you that the people take the booty to their homes and you take Allah's Apostle to your homes? If the Ansar took their way through a valley or a mountain pass, I would take the Ansar's valley or a mountain pass... And but for the migration, I would have been one of the Ansar.'

SubhanAllah. May Allah ﷻ accept my intention to take after the great people of Ansar whose noble intentions were to look after the Muhajiroon in their time of dire need. What a blessing to have the Messenger of Allah praise the Ansar, and identify himself as being one of the Ansar, in such a beautiful way!

Furthermore, I'd like to thank my first family, for always believing in me, you are, by far my greatest cheerleaders (and also my most eagle-eyed critics)! Thanks, Dad, Mum, *Baji* Sam, Haani and Hasib (in age order!). You are all a huge gift from Allah ﷻ and my (secret) source of never ending inspiration and motivation, alhamdulillah.

I'd like to thank my loving, caring husband, Abid, who is as much a realist as I am a dreamer. Thank you for balancing me, completing me and for your words of wisdom and advice when I have needed them the most.

To my lovely children... What can I say? Fatimah, Abbas, Ziyad, Zayd and Rida. You give me challenges and upheavals amidst all the joy; life would truly be boring without you! Thank you for understanding and being patient when Mum's head is in the clouds (or her eyes are firmly placed on her laptop, striving to meet writing deadlines!). Always remember to dream big and then work really hard!

To my wonderful friends, and each and every reader of my blog, I have felt honoured by your presence and your company on this journey. Without you, my lovely readers, and Allah's pure Generosity, I wouldn't have had the audacity to write this book! Thank you for giving a place for my voice to reside.

Alhamdulillah, I've been blessed to have had many a mentor and guide on my early writing journey. Farhana Shaikh, founder of Dahlia publishing and The AsianWriter, was one of the first and I'd like to thank her for being my first official writing mentor in my adult life. And I'd like to thank you from all of us you inspire, for working tirelessly to allow the Asian voice to resound in this noisy world.

To everyone at Beacon Books, thank you for making my dream possible, especially Brother Jamil for sharing my dream to write a self-development book for all Muslim women out there, and to Siema for her help in turning my many blog posts into a book! Thank you for all the questions that helped me delve deeper into the message I was trying to convey.

My writing life wouldn't be complete without my writing buddies: Nabeela, Nazira, Sarah, Mala, Sujana and Anita. Thank you for your endless support and encouragement. This journey would be a long, lonely and tremulous one without you!

Love and duas to all, please keep me in your blessed prayers.

Please do keep in touch at *7ofus.blog*, Sidra Ansari via Facebook, peace.prayer.love on Instagram and @sidra_writes on Twitter. Remember how much I love to hear stories! When I hear from my readers, it gives me purpose and so I thank Allah ﷻ for each and every one of you. For without a reader, there is no book...

Was Salaam,
Sidra <3